Preventing the School-to-Prison Pipeline

Preventing the School-to-Prison Pipeline is the first book written to provide school psychologists and other K–12 mental health professionals with knowledge and strategies intended to help them disrupt the criminalization of historically oppressed learners in today's classrooms. A phenomenon of the United States' intersecting education and criminal justice systems, the school-to-prison pipeline is the process by which school staff punish already marginalized or at-risk students—primarily Black youth—in ways that enable a lifetime of targeting by police, court, and carceral operations. Exploring the unmet needs of students with mental, emotional, and behavioral health disorders, the effects of implicit and explicit bias, adverse school and court policies, and other biopsychosocial factors, this powerful book offers a preventative, public-health approach to providing clinical care to vulnerable students without compromising school safety. School psychologists, counselors, and social workers will come away with urgent and actionable insights into advocacy, collaboration, preventive interventions, alternative discipline measures in schools, and more.

Charles Bartholomew is a certified school psychologist and a licensed psychologist in the State of Georgia, USA.

Preventing the School-to-Prison Pipeline

A Public Health Approach for School Psychologists, Counselors, and Social Workers

Charles Bartholomew

Routledge
Taylor & Francis Group
NEW YORK AND LONDON

Designed cover image: Getty images

First published 2023
by Routledge
605 Third Avenue, New York, NY 10158

and by Routledge
4 Park Square, Milton Park, Abingdon, Oxon, OX14 4RN

Routledge is an imprint of the Taylor & Francis Group, an informa business

© 2023 Charles Bartholomew

Library of Congress Cataloging-in-Publication Data
Names: Bartholomew, Charles (School psychologist), author.
Title: Preventing the school-to-prison pipeline : a public health approach for school psychologists, counselors, and social workers / Charles Bartholomew.
Identifiers: LCCN 2022049490 (print) | LCCN 2022049491 (ebook) | ISBN 9781032254906 (hardback) | ISBN 9781032256511 (paperback) | ISBN 9781003284383 (ebook)
Subjects: LCSH: School-to-prison pipeline—United States. | School discipline—Social aspects—United States. | School violence—United States—Prevention. | African American youth—Education—Social aspects. | School mental health services—United States. | School psychology—United States.
Classification: LCC LB3012.2 .B37 2023 (print) | LCC LB3012.2 (ebook) | DDC 371.50973—dc23/eng/20221220
LC record available at https://lccn.loc.gov/2022049490
LC ebook record available at https://lccn.loc.gov/2022049491

ISBN: 978-1-032-25490-6 (hbk)
ISBN: 978-1-032-25651-1 (pbk)
ISBN: 978-1-003-28438-3 (ebk)

DOI: 10.4324/9781003284383

Typeset in Adobe Caslon Pro
by Apex CoVantage, LLC

Access the Support Material: www.routledge.com/9781032256511

This book is dedicated to my parents, who knew very little about books except that they could not read them. My parents and their children were all born into the peonage system, which continued for almost one hundred years after being outlawed by the U.S. Congress in 1867. It continued to flourish in the South and made millionaires from the cheap labor of former slaves. For generations, my family was paid too little to escape poverty or the indebtedness to the plantation stores, too poor to leave the plantations to seek gainful employment in other parts of the country, and too afraid to challenge the status quo that continued to reap benefits from the remnants of an alliance between government power and slave-based agriculture and Jim Crow laws. In the sugar cane fields outside of New Orleans, federal troops teamed up with French planters in 1811 to fight slave rebels, culminating in the largest slave revolt in American history. This "unholy alliance," as Rasmussen (2011) called it, would come to define the young American nation as a slave country in the years leading up to the Civil War. My parents were born about one hundred years after this rebellion but within the same repressive community. No words or acts of gratitude can ever be enough to thank them and the countless brave white, black, brown, and red men and women who were willing to sacrifice everything (including their lives) so the ideals of America could be realized and a man like me could be literate and free!

CONTENTS

PREFACE

Over the past few decades, exemplary mental and behavioral health research studies and publications have surfaced in the mental health community about risk factors that can leave school-aged children susceptible to a variety of problems. These risk factors are pervasive and represent urgent challenges for children and their parents, teachers, mental health providers, and/or social justice advocates. Many of these factors also disproportionately affect African American children and adolescents with mental, emotional, and behavioral health (MEB) difficulties and frequently exacerbate systemic inequalities that are present in their lives. Some of these youth enter what is currently called the school-to-prison pipeline, from which there is little chance of escaping.

The rate of incarceration of all youth in the United States is higher than any other industrialized country in the world (The Annie E. Casey Foundation, 2021), which should be alarming to every American. This rate is, however, not an equal opportunity problem. African American youth are more than four times as likely to be detained or committed in juvenile facilities as their White peers. Nationally, the overall youth placement rate in 2021 was 114 per 100,000, according to The Sentencing Project (2021). The African American youth rate, however, was 315 per 100,000, compared to the White youth placement rate of 72 per 100,000. Although African American youth comprised only 15% of all youth across the United States when these data were examined, they constituted 41% of youth in placement.

While articles and books published by the American Psychological Association (APA), National Association of School Psychologists (NASP), and other research journals have made significant contributions to our understanding of factors associated with the school-to-prison pipeline (e.g., prevention, ethics, the components of a biopsychosocial practice, zero tolerance policies and procedures in the public school, and the impact that racism has on African Americans), most references to the pipeline have remained fragmented and certainly without the sense of urgency this issue requires. There are also multiple publications that focus on the legal aspects of the school-to-prison problem (e.g., *Deconstructing the School-to-Prison Pipeline: New Directions for Youth Development*, 2003; *Disrupting the School-to-Prison Pipeline*, 2012; and *The School-to-Prison Pipeline: A Comprehensive Assessment*, 2016), but these resources are typically about court-level practices or rehabilitation and lack the in-depth mental, emotional, and behavioral health components necessary for a comprehensive prevention and intervention plan or strategy.

The focus on rehabilitation, fragmentation in the literature, and lack of in-depth mental, emotional, and behavioral health components are believed, in part, to be the result of the unique and complex nature of this pipeline. The school-to-prison pipeline (STPP) is impacted by many institutions, particularly the schools and the courts. It is also impacted by social conditions, such as poverty, culture, family background and structure, community, and access to medical/mental health care, as well as by biological and psychological factors, such as one's developmental status and mental health, personality, temperament and resilience, and the social construct we call race (Gannon, 2016). One of the first individuals to address these dynamics and their relevance to psychology was the University of Rochester internist and psychoanalyst George Engel. In 1977, Engel proposed that biological, psychological, and sociocultural influences are inextricably intertwined, and that we should use the biopsychosocial approach to behavioral health care to address these dynamics. Because of this perspective, behavioral health care's use of the biopsychosocial approach is ideally suited for understanding, preventing, interrupting, and even dismantling many of those forces that funnel school-aged children into the school-to-prison pipeline.

This book examines how biopsychosocial factors, such as court- and school-level practices, the unmet needs of youth with mental, emotional, and behavioral health disorders, and explicit and implicit bias, fuel the pipeline. It recommends the use of the biopsychosocial approach to behavioral healthcare, which is focused on prevention and explains how preventive interventions can be provided within the public school setting (e.g., Schoolwide positive behavior interventions and supports, multi-tiered systems of support) without reducing school safety. It also provides compelling scientific evidence of the need for ongoing advocacy efforts, collaboration, preventive interventions, research, alternative discipline measures in schools, and objective social discourse.

The recognition of the need for advocacy and social justice in psychology has gained momentum over the past decade (Chen, 2013). Although research studies, discussions, and proactive efforts in these areas have sometimes been hijacked by politicians and the media for various gains, psychology has a history of advocating for troubled youth and providing research-based treatments and interventions. It is a leading contributor to understanding child and adolescent mental health development and the risk factors that often compromise this process. It is an advocate for youth in schools and society in general, especially those youth who have historically been disenfranchised or marginalized because of race and ethnicity, culture, socioeconomic status, disabilities, and sexual and gender identity and orientation. It has helped society develop an understanding of how cognitions, emotions, and behaviors change and how subtle and sometimes aggressive efforts can positively or adversely make long- and short-term differences in the lives of youth. Most important, however, has been psychology's contribution to society's understanding of preventive methods at the individual, familial, and systemic levels, which has shaped new approaches to a host of developmental, social, mental, and behavioral health problems. As Romano (2015) indicated in his book *Prevention Psychology*, this profession, in partnership with other disciplines and specialties, is designed to prevent problems and strengthen individual and community protections against personal and psychological distress.

As indicated earlier, the STPP is a complex problem. For readability purposes, the chapters of this book are first separated into sections that address similar themes or issues. Section I (The School-to-Prison Pipeline) examines what the STPP is and how this pipeline funnels youth into what Golash-Boza (2019), Selman and Leighton (2010), and other scholars call the prison-industrial complex. Section II (How Adverse Practices "Fuel" the Pipeline) examines how individual and systemic factors such as the unmet needs of youth with mental, emotional, and behavioral health disorders; explicit and implicit bias; and school-level practices "fuel" the STPP. Section III (Transformative Practices) introduces the biopsychosocial approach to behavioral health care, which has been described as both a philosophy of clinical care (Borrell-Carrió et al., 2004) and the clinical application of behavioral science and ethics to behavioral health needs (Melchert, 2015). Section IV (Prevention: A Moral and Ethical Imperative) examines how public schools have become the de facto mental health system for troubled youth and how school mental health professionals (e.g., school psychologists, school counselors, and school social workers), in partnership with community health and mental health professionals, are becoming increasingly involved in mental health promotion, prevention, and treatment. Section V (Mapping an Agenda for the Future of All Youth) was written as several medical, psychological, and sociological events were unfolding simultaneously in the United States. These events include the Coronavirus Disease 2019 (COVID-19), COVID-19's disproportionate and devastating impact on African Americans, and the recent killings of several unarmed, innocent African Americans. The impact of these events is discussed as it relates to preventing the school-to-prison pipeline.

ACKNOWLEDGEMENTS

After being employed for several years in a long-term psychiatric facility in the 80s, I got my first job as a school psychologist. This job was primarily in a juvenile facility/prison, but I also visited adult prisons since there were teenagers and young men under the age of 21 there also. I traveled throughout the state identifying students with prior special education eligibility. I was amazed by the number of children, teenagers, and young adults who were incarcerated and the overrepresentation of African Americans in this population. This job was followed by additional graduate school studies, which were encouraged by two of my mentors (A.C. Blanks, PhD, and Jerzy Wysocki, MD), and ultimately a PhD in psychology (school emphasis) from the University of Southern Mississippi.

This book has taken me over 40 years to research, conceptualize, and write, largely because there was initially little research available about the school-to-prison pipeline (STPP), mental health prevention, and the components of a biopsychosocial practice. Discussions and recommendations by colleagues and the publication of Prevention Psychology (John L. Romano, PhD) and Biopsychosocial Practice (Timothy P. Melchert, PhD), both in 2015, caught my attention. These discussions and books were invaluable in helping me conceptualize the STPP as a complex biopsychosocial problem to which psychological science must respond.

In addition to working in various clinical/school settings and having met or interacted with many brilliant clinicians, scholars, academicians, and researchers, I have also consulted with hundreds of teachers (who are frequently on the front line of every innovative practice involving children), school counselors, social workers, principals, friends, and even parents about this book. Many provided brief one- or two-word recommendations or responses, but many others critiqued my book's chapters, made recommendations, or suggested other research studies or collaborators I should consider. Unfortunately, I was never successful in securing a coauthor but still gained very useful evaluation and feedback.

I am certain that I have missed acknowledging someone in this book, which I sincerely regret and extend my apologizes. But to identify those that I can remember, I must include my editors, Sarah Schelkoph and Daniel Schwartz, friends, colleagues, academicians, researchers, scholars, and practitioners from throughout the country, who include Charles Barrett, PhD, Janine Jones, PhD, Scott Graves, PhD, Timothy P. Melchert, PhD, Samuel Song, PhD, Jennifer F. Kelly, PhD, Kelsie Reed, PhD, Susan Jung, EdS, Virginia Hinton, EdD, Telsie A. Davis, PhD, Brenda Dumas, MA, Delores Spencer-Izegbu, EdD, Deborah Staniszewski, PhD, Ted Wiggins, BA, Shelisse Sims, MA, Cicely Keller, MA, Ma'at Smith (College Student), Nichole Murray, PhD, R. Steve McCallum, PhD, Tim Bailey, Francine Bailey, BA, Edmond Franklin, BS, DMD, Carlotta Franklin, BS, Cherylle Bartholomew, MA, Gina M. Hudson, PhD, and Charles E. Carter, Jr., MA. Without their support, this book would have never been written. Also included in this acknowledgment are my mentors, Andrea Wesley, PhD, Augustus C. Blanks, PhD, Jerzy Wysocki, MD, Rev. Wilmer Todd, and immediate family members, who have been a source of encouragement and support throughout my life.

I must also include institutions such as Richmond County School System, Richmond County Juvenile Court, Community Treatment Center, Augusta, Georgia, The State of Georgia, Georgia Department of Juvenile Justice, and Richmond County Government, who provided in-kind support or funding to The CSRA Transitional Center, Inc., a grassroots community-based diversion program for at-risk youth. This program was also supported by volunteers and the funds of countless individuals who championed this grassroots effort. Most importantly, I'd like to recognize the University of Southern Mississippi and Nicholls State University, where I obtained my terminal and Master's/Bachelor's degrees, respectively, and Southern University, Louisiana State University, and the University of Kentucky, where I was always welcomed as an itinerant student, and the Junior Auxiliary, who helped fund my graduate school education.

A long-awaited apology is also in order to the volunteers from the Speech Communication, Speech Pathology, and Linguistics departments at the University of Southern Mississippi and psychologists throughout this country who participated in my research study. This was in 1987, and this study became the topic of my dissertation, which is referenced in this book. I will be, forever, grateful for your assistance. My sincere apology for taking so long to acknowledge your support and say thanks!

The great things about this book I owe almost entirely to the individuals listed previously and the research studies referenced, while the errors, omissions, and unvarnished statements and conclusions are exclusively mine.

References

The Annie E. Casey Foundation. (2021). *Youth residing in juvenile detention, correctional and/or residential facilities in the United States*. https://datacenter.kidscount.org/data/line/42-youth-residing-in-juvenile-detention-correctional-and-or-residential-facilities#1/any/false/1729,871,573,36,867,133,18,17,14,12/asc/any/17599

Bahena, S., Cooc, N., Currie-Rubin, R., Kuttner, P., & Ng, M. (2012). Disrupting the school-to-prison pipeline. *Harvard Educational Review*, 2012.

Borrell-Carrió, F., Suchman, A., & Epstein, R. (2004). The biopsychosocial model 25 years later: Principles, practice, and scientific inquiry. *The Annals of Family Medicine*, *2*(6), 576–582. https://doi.org/10.1370/afm.245

Chen, E. C. (2013, April 1). Multicultural competence and social justice advocacy in group psychology and group psychotherapy. *The Group Psychologist*, https://www.apadivisions.org/division-49/publications/newsletter/group-psychologist/2013/04/multicultural-competence

Engel, G. L. (1977, April 8). The need for a new medical model: A challenge for biomedicine. *Science*, *196*(4286), 129–136. https://doi.org/10.1126/science.847460. PMID: 847460.

Gannon, M. (2016). Race is a social construct, scientists argue. *Scientific American*.

Golash-Boza, T. M. (2019). *Race & racisms: A critical approach*. Oxford University Press.

Mallett, C. A. (2016). *The school-to-prison pipeline, a comprehensive assessment*. Springer Publishing Company.

Melchert, T. P. (2015). *Biopsychosocial practice: A science-based framework for behavioral healthcare*. American Psychological Association.

Rasmussen, D. (2011). *American uprising: The untold story of America's largest slave revolt*. HarperCollins Publishers.

Romano, J. L. (2015). *Prevention psychology: Enhancing personal and social wellbeing.* American Psychological Association.

Selman, D., & Leighton, P. (2010). *Punishment for sale: Private prisons, big business, and the incarceration binge.* Rowman & Littlefield.

The Sentencing Project. (2021, July). *Black disparities in youth incarceration.* www.sentenc ingproject.org/publications/black-disparities-youth-incarceration/

Wald, M., & Losen, D. J. (2003). *Deconstructing the school-to-prison pipeline: New directions for youth development.* Jossey-Bass.

SECTION I
THE SCHOOL-TO-PRISON PIPELINE

1

FUNNELING CHILDREN INTO THE PRISON INDUSTRIAL COMPLEX

The school-to-prison pipeline is best understood as a set of school policies and practices that make it more likely for students to face criminal involvement with the juvenile courts than to attain a quality education (Mallett, 2016). It has been described as a national concern and an epidemic, and the NAACP (NAACP Legal Defense and Educational Fund, n.d.) has called it one of the most urgent challenges in education today. Generally, the school-to-prison pipeline refers to systemic setbacks that gradually steer students away from positive school connections and academic success and toward increasing criminal activity. The school-to-prison pipeline (STPP) is frequently considered a recent phenomenon in the United States (Mallett, 2016); however, this is incorrect! The United States has a long and heinous history of detaining and incarcerating African Americans dating back to chattel slavery, lynch laws, and convict lease and peonage systems. The STPP has frequently been misconstrued by the public as soft on crime and hard on the criminal justice system, but this too is incorrect. This pipeline is about the disproportionate incarceration of African American children, frequently for the same behaviors as White children, and the inequities and biopsychosocial factors that frequently "fuel" this process.

The STPP is a unique and complex problem in the US largely because it is impacted by many institutions, particularly the schools and the courts.

DOI: 10.4324/9781003284383-2

It is also impacted by social conditions (e.g., poverty, culture, family background and structure, community, and access to medical/mental health care) and biological and psychological factors (e.g., one's developmental status and mental health, personality, temperament and resilience, and the social construct we call race).

History of the School-to-Prison Pipeline

The public school system in the United States, as we know it today, is a relatively new endeavor. It was not until 1918 that all states passed laws requiring children to attend at least elementary school, and it took almost one hundred years (from 1900 to 1996) for the percentage of teenagers who graduated from high school to increase from about 6% to about 85%. Although the first African Americans arrived as slaves in the colonies in 1619, their education remained very low until Lincoln issued the Emancipation Proclamation in 1863. Their literacy rate did not rise to 70% until 1910, largely because Southern states favored slavery over the education of African Americans (Thattai, 2017). During the 19th and

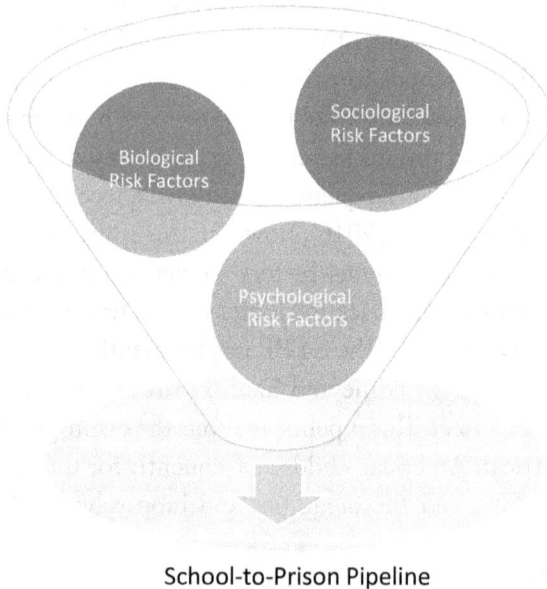

Biological
Risk Factors

Sociological
Risk Factors

Psychological
Risk Factors

School-to-Prison Pipeline

Figure 1.1 School-to-Prison Pipeline

most of the 20th centuries, schools in the United States focused primarily on academic and learning needs. This was separate from the juvenile courts, which were established during the late 19th century and dedicated their first 80 years to the rehabilitation of offenders, truants, and other wayward young people. Over the past 30 years, however, this separation of duties and responsibilities between schools and the juvenile court system has shifted, and both institutions have simultaneously moved toward punitive policies and practices. These punitive policies have affected how schools and juvenile courts work (Mallett, 2016).

In schools, students' academic and learning needs have remained a priority, but increasing discipline has become a major factor in the overall management of schools. For example, of the 49 million students in the United States who enrolled in the 2011–2012 academic year, 3.5 million students were suspended in school, 3.45 million students were suspended out of school, and 130,000 students were expelled (U.S. Department of Education, 2022).

The juvenile justice system in the United States is the primary system currently used to handle minors who are convicted of criminal offenses. This is an evolving system, however, whose mission has changed dramatically over the past 300 years. Throughout the 17th and 18th centuries, few legal differences existed between children and adults, and even children as young as six or seven could receive the death penalty. In 1899, the first juvenile court was formed in Illinois with the underlying assumption that juveniles were more amenable to rehabilitation than adult criminals. Although this assumption continues to prevail, debates about juvenile court's effectiveness and criticisms focused on racial discrimination and discrimination toward children with mental health problems or learning disabilities have surfaced (American juvenile justice system, 2009). During the 1970s, attempts were implemented to address some of these concerns through community-based programs, diversion, and alternative approaches, but these attempts were short-lived due to the rising crime rates of the 1960s and media misrepresentation of this crime throughout the 1970s and 80s (Snyder & Sickmund, 1999). This paved the way for President Reagan's War on Drugs and subsequent "tough-on-crime" policies for juvenile crime (Butts & Travis, 2002).

In the 1990s, juvenile crime, especially violent crime, decreased, but policies remained the same. Many schools and politicians adopted zero tolerance policies with regard to crime and argued that rehabilitative approaches were less effective than strict punishment. Get-tough advocates supported the merger between the adult criminal and juvenile systems by expanding the scope of transfer provisions or waivers that brought children under the jurisdiction of the adult criminal system. Some states moved specific classes of crimes from juvenile court to adult criminal court, while others gave this power to judges or prosecutors on a case-by-case basis. Still others allowed the courts to treat offending youth like adults but within the juvenile system. In addition, juvenile courts were transformed to allow for prosecution of juveniles more easily as adults; at the same time, the adult system was redefining which acts constituted a serious crime. The "Three Strikes Law," which was first implemented on March 7, 1994, fundamentally altered the criminal offenses that resulted in detention, imprisonment, and even life sentences for both youth and adults. The purpose of these laws was to drastically increase punishment of those convicted of more than two serious crimes. Although not specific to juvenile offenders, the Three Strikes Law was enacted during a period when the lines between juvenile and adult courts were becoming increasingly blurred ("American Juvenile Justice System," 2009).

One example of the tough-on-crime policy that contributed to the increased number of young people being arrested and detained is the Gun-Free Schools Act (GFSA) in 1994. This act was intended to prosecute young offenders for serious crimes, such as gun possession on school property, but many states interpreted this law to include less dangerous weapons and drug possession. Many schools even interpret the GFSA to include infractions that pose no safety concerns, such as disobeying school rules, insubordination, and disruption. These offenses can now warrant school suspension, expulsion, and involvement with juvenile courts, which makes many schools the primary setting for juvenile arrests ("American Juvenile Justice System," 2009).

Schools and Juvenile Courts—A Precarious Alliance

In 2010, more than 2.1 million youth under the age of 18 were arrested. This resulted in the juvenile courts handling almost 1.3 million delinquency cases, which was a 17% increase since 1985. Additionally, the juvenile courts processed nearly 150,000 status offender cases, which are acts that are only illegal for minors and not for adults, representing a slight increase since the mid-1990s. Policymakers, administrators, practitioners, and teachers do not intentionally try to harm children and adolescents in schools or in juvenile justice settings, and most focus their decisions on the best interests of these youth. However, hundreds of thousands of middle and high school students are caught every year within the STPP through suspensions, arrests by school resource officers (SROs), and expulsions. A single suspension or expulsion from school doubles the risk of a student repeating a grade, which is also a strong risk factor for the student dropping out of high school and becoming involved in the juvenile justice system. For example, in a longitudinal study of one million Texas students, it was revealed that a student who is suspended or expelled for a discretionary violation is nearly three times more likely to be in contact with the juvenile justice system the following year. Schools and juvenile courts were never intended to operate in tandem; nevertheless, a partnership between them has developed through a punitive and harmful framework involving court referrals, probation, and placement in juvenile or adult correctional facilities (Mallett, 2016).

A number of factors have impacted both schools and juvenile courts, leading to today's punitive paradigm. A review of all of these factors is beyond the scope of this publication, but the following nationwide changes were of particular influence because of the movement in the 1980s and 1990s toward a tough-on-crime approach in both adult and juvenile courts. This was made evident by the "three strikes and you're out" laws and the large numbers of youthful offenders transferred to adult criminal courts, rising rates of juvenile arrests for violent crimes in the 1980s, and concerns, though incorrect, that young people were increasingly dangerous. As a result, many behaviors that adults once saw as innocent teenage pranks were seen as violent and requiring Juvenile Court intervention. This also encouraged the passage and enactment of the Gun-Free Schools Act of 1994, which requires local educational agencies in each state receiving federal funds to expel, for at least one year, any student who brings a firearm or weapon to school; schools are also directed to develop policies requiring the referral of these students to the criminal justice or juvenile delinquency system). In addition, the impact and aftermath of the 1999 Columbine school shooting, and subsequent school shootings, made many parents hypervigilant about the safety of their children in school (Mallett, 2016).

Four additional factors that have led to today's punitive paradigm include the establishment of zero tolerance disciplinary policies across most schools nationwide, the increased utilization and federal funding of police officers in schools, declining school funding, and the resegregation of schools by race and class (Mallett, 2016). The implementation of these factors is largely discretionary and based on state and county rules and practices; therefore, they are more suitably addressed in Chapter 3.

One of the most prolific writers about the school-to-prison pipeline is Christopher A. Mallett, a professor of social work and a licensed social worker and attorney. According to Mallett, this shift in schools and the juvenile court system toward punitive policies and practices has been detrimental to many vulnerable children and adolescents. Most of these individuals already face complicated problems and poor long-term outcomes. These problems can include poverty, trauma, and mental health difficulties, all of which frequently warrant their own specific interventions for the child or adolescent to function optimally in society (2016). Furthermore, school punishments are not equitably distributed, even though zero tolerance disciplinary policies have attempted to standardize consequences for unruly children and adolescents in most schools. This means that low-income students, for example, are much more likely to be punished in school than others (Skiba et al., 2002; Skiba et al., 2011) and almost all young people who end up in the nation's detention and incarceration facilities have troubled lives.

Trauma, as already mentioned, is a potentially significant vulnerability for children and adolescents. Most children and adolescents in the United States do not suffer from or experience violent traumas or mental health problems. However, reviews of detained and incarcerated youthful offenders have found significantly higher incidences of these experiences among young people who end up in the nation's detention and incarceration facilities (Mallett, 2016). The first large-scale longitudinal study of the mental health needs and outcomes of juvenile detainees was conducted by Teplin et al. in 2013. This study found that exposure to trauma is common among juvenile detainees. Of the 1,829 randomly selected youth who were arrested and detained between 1995 and 1998 in Cook County, IL, 93% of the participants experienced one or more traumas in their lifetime, and more than 1 in 10 detainees met diagnostic criteria for post-traumatic stress disorder during the year prior to their interview. Of this group, 46% of the males and 57% of the females had two or more psychiatric disorders.

Ironically, most of the young people who are involved in the discipline system as a result of harsher punitive policies and practices actually pose little or no threat to other students, their schools, or their communities. Many of the children and adolescents are involved for many reasons, such as home difficulties, violence, school problems, peer troubles, offending activities, status offenses, and children services agency involvement (Mallett, 2016). In school systems, particularly those schools that are overburdened and underfinanced, many students have been increasingly suspended and expelled due to the criminalizing of both typical adolescent developmental behaviors and low-level-type misdemeanors, such as acting out in class, truancy, fighting, disobedience, and other similar offenses (U. S. Department of Education, 2022). These suspensions and expulsions frequently lead to referrals to juvenile court, adjudication, and probation supervision, all of which have the potential to capture students within the STPP. If the pipeline is not disrupted or a young person does not do well while on probation or supervision by the court, detention and/or incarceration may occur. In its seminal study, *Are Zero Tolerance Policies Effective in the Schools? An Evidentiary Review and Recommendations*, the American Psychological Association Zero Tolerance Task Force wrote, "It seems conceptually likely that school suspension and expulsion constitute the critical links between school zero tolerance policies and students' involvement in the juvenile justice system" (2008, p. 79).

Developmental models of children with conduct disorders and juvenile delinquency suggest a similar link. As at-risk youth become alienated from school through suspensions and expulsions, they increasingly seek out other antisocial peers. Frequently, this accelerates their course toward juvenile offending and puts them at greater risk for delinquent behavior and subsequent incarceration when placed unsupervised on the streets of the community for days or weeks at a time (American Psychological Association Zero Tolerance Task Force, 2008).

Rehabilitation, Prevention, and Mental Health Promotion

The terms rehabilitation and prevention have frequently been misunderstood and confused by the public, especially when discussing students who have been caught within the STPP due to typical adolescent developmental behaviors and low-level-type misdemeanors. These terms, however, are vastly different processes. In this context, rehabilitation is based on a restorative process, such as training or therapy after an illegal offense has been committed. Prevention, on the other hand, refers to intervening in a potential problem or behavior before it actually occurs. Mental health promotion can be distinguished from prevention by its focus on healthy outcomes, such as competence and well-being. In addition, many of these outcomes, such as prosocial involvement, spirituality, and social justice, are intrinsically valued in their own right (Catalano et al., 2004; Sandler, 2007). Mental health promotion interventions are usually targeted to the general public and are designed to enhance individuals' ability to achieve developmentally appropriate tasks and a positive self-esteem and to strengthen their ability to cope with adversity (The National Research Council and the Institute of Medicine, 2009).

The Bureau of Justice Statistics (BJS) collects data on police-public contact for youth between the ages of 16–24 but does not have data on youth under 16 years. According to the BJS, youth between the ages of 16–24 years are more likely to experience contact with the police than members of any other age group. However, this contact may be youth initiated, police initiated, an arrest, or the result of the youth being a victim (Development Services Group, Inc., 2018). Arrests are only a small portion of the interactions that occur between police and youth (Goodrich et al., 2014), but police officers are the first juvenile justice decision-makers to encounter youth (Development Services Group, Inc., 2018). As is indicated earlier, schools are the primary setting for juvenile arrests ("American Juvenile Justice System," 2009).

Options for law enforcement, or the police, when making a decision about the commission of an illegal juvenile offense typically include questioning, which can be followed by a "rehabilitative" effort, such as a warning, community release to the parent, taking the youth to the police station and recording the offense, referring the youth to a diversion program, issuing a citation, making a formal referral to juvenile court, or taking the youth to a detention center or group home (Lawrence & Hemmens, 2008). As is indicated earlier, the decision to refer the youthful offender to diversion services during the 1970s was short lived, not because scientific studies indicated that these services do not work, but because of the rising crime rates of the 1960s and media misrepresentation of this crime throughout the 1970s and 80s (Snyder & Sickmund, 1999). Diversion services can be a critical component in the rehabilitative or prevention process for troubled youth in disrupting the STPP.

If law enforcement decides that diversion services are appropriate as a rehabilitative or preventive effort, these services may be offered by the juvenile court or a community-based agency and entail a wide array of alternatives, including teen or youth court, truancy intervention programs, respite, shelter care, mentoring, curfew enforcement programs, parent training, restorative justice, and other alternatives. Two examples of these alternatives include the following programs:

- The project Back-on-Track, which is an after-school diversion program designed for low- and mid-level youthful offenders. One-year follow-up evaluations found that this program significantly decreased the recidivism rate for participants when compared to nonparticipating youthful offenders with similar offending histories (Myers et al., 2000).
- The CSRA Transitional Center, Inc., which is an after-school, research-based, collaborative diversion program involving the public school system, mental health, and juvenile court. Low- and mid-level youthful offenders who are at risk for continued problems in school, home, or in the community are targeted and provided an array of services, including case management, intake/risk needs assessment, recreational activities, and counseling. Eighty-five percent of the youth who completed the "Ninety-Day Diversion Program" did not return to juvenile court after one year, and this program sparked the development of other diversion programs throughout the state for at-risk youth. This program was

the first demonstration project in the state developed and implemented by a school psychologist (Nastasi et al., 1997).

In addition to the diversion examples already mentioned is the *Juvenile Diversion Guidebook*, which was published in 2011. This guidebook is a research-based project whose effort was to create successful and replicable models of juvenile justice reform through targeted investments in key states of Illinois, Louisiana, Pennsylvania, and Washington, and through action networks focusing on key issues in California, Colorado, Connecticut, Florida, Kansas, Maryland, Massachusetts, New Jersey, North Carolina, Ohio, Texas, and Wisconsin. This guidebook seeks to accelerate progress toward a more effective, fair, and developmentally sound juvenile justice system that holds young people accountable for their actions, provides for their rehabilitation, protects them from harm, increases their life chances, and manages the risks they pose to themselves and to the public. This research-based project has a 16-step model for developing and improving juvenile courts' diversion programs. This 16-step model includes, for example, the type of diversions to utilize and how to determine eligibility, meet legal mandates, and determine effectiveness and fidelity (Models for Change, 2011).

One of the earliest studies about the STPP was conducted by Wald and Losen in 2003 (*Deconstructing the School-to-Prison Pipeline: New Directions for Youth Development*) and was followed by Bahena et al., 2012 (*Disrupting the School-to-Prison Pipeline*). However, Mallett's (2016) book, *The School-to-Prison Pipeline: A Comprehensive Assessment*, consolidated many of the salient features of these and other publications and provides a comprehensive assessment of this problem. In particular, Mallett addresses some of the challenges faced by school-aged youth who enter the STPP and how stakeholders in the schools, juvenile justice systems, and policy arenas can find effective rehabilitative alternatives to solve pipeline problems. His ideas are captured in this poignant statement:

> Today's punitive paradigm across schools and juvenile courts is significant cause for concern not only because of the grave impact that tough-on-crime juvenile justice policies and zero tolerance-focused schools have on the health and well-being

of young people but also because of the secondary and tertiary problems affiliated with these policies and the poor long-term outcomes for many students. Although there is limited movement away from these punishment-focused policies, ongoing and increased action within school districts and juvenile courts must be pursued. Otherwise, another generation of at-risk children and adolescents will be significantly harmed. For many, this damage is permanent.

(2016, p. 7)

Mallett's assessment of the STPP is exemplary in its overview of the scope of this problem and has been an invaluable resource in the completion of this book. However, he emphasized only rehabilitative strategies after a juvenile has committed an offense. Prevention is not a new concept in mental health, and the field of prevention has now developed to the point where reduction of risk, prevention of onset, and early intervention are realistic possibilities (U. S. Department of Health and Human Services, 1999). According to Nation et al. (2003), successful preventive interventions are typically theory-driven, culturally relevant, developmentally appropriate, and delivered across multiple contexts. Prevention also addresses the importance of risk and protective factors, advocacy, and social justice efforts (Albee, 1996; Vera & Kenny, 2013). Organizations such as the American Psychological Association (APA) and the National Association of School Psychologists (NASP) have been forerunners in advocating for early interventions for troubled youth for decades and have made significant contributions to the public's understanding of the biological, psychological, social, and behavioral health correlates that put children and adolescents at risk. As is seen later in subsequent chapters, however, prevention science is underutilized.

Disproportionate Impact on African American Youth

One particular risk factor that is inextricably linked to the STPP is the race of the child or adolescent. Despite progress the United States has made in the past fifty years in trying to eradicate racism and racial discrimination, one of the most pressing problems that is associated with the STPP is the disproportionate impact it has had on African American youth. Racial disparities in the application of school discipline in public schools have been documented for many years, and these disparities most frequently result in juvenile court referrals of African American youth (Wald & Kurlaender, 2003). Therefore, since African American children and adolescents are disproportionately affected in comparison to other races, the school-to-prison pipeline is best viewed within the context of the social construct called race (Gannon, 2016).

According to federal classifications, the four most recognized racial groups in the United States are African Americans (Blacks), American Indians and Alaska Natives, Asian Americans and Pacific Islanders, and White Americans (Whites). Hispanic American (Latino) is an ethnicity, but it may apply to a person of any race. The U.S. Office of Management and Budget outlined these broad racial categories in 1978 but included the many distinct ethnic subgroups within each of the broad categories. For example, Asian Americans and Pacific Islanders include 43 ethnic groups who speak over 100 languages and dialects, and White Americans include innumerable cultural, ethnic, and social subgroups and encompass the span of immigration from the 1400s to the 21st century. It should also be noted that, because slavery brought African Americans from many different parts of the continent of Africa, African Americans have their own innumerable cultural, ethnic, and social subgroups as well.

Individuals whose racial and/or ethnic background is visibly identifiable encounter more discrimination than those who are perceived as White (U.S. Department of Housing and Urban Development, 2012). For more than three decades, African American male students have been particularly affected by exclusionary school disciplinary practices, such as office referrals, suspensions, school-based arrests, alternative learning environments, and expulsions (Achilles et al., 2007; Skiba et al., 2002). In 2012, the U.S. Department of Education identified that, in school districts with more than 50,000 students, African American students represented 24% of enrollment but 35% of on-campus arrests (McCurdy, 2014). This discrepancy was found even after controlling for other explanations, such as misbehavior, academic performance, attitudes, parental attention, school characteristics, and socioeconomic status (Carter, 2005; Kupchik, 2012). A 2009–2010 survey of 72,000 schools (kindergarten through high school) also showed that while African American students made up only 18% of those enrolled in the schools sampled, they accounted for 35% of those suspended once and 46% of those suspended more than once (Rudd, 2014). Data indicate that even African American preschoolers are three to five times more likely to be expelled from school than their Asian American, Latino, and White peers (Cokley et al., 2014). If African American students are not in school, they cannot learn, they fall behind socially and academically, and they are often left unsupervised and without constructive activities in environments filled with negative influences. All these factors put them at a greater risk for entering the STPP.

References

Achilles, G. M., Mclaughlin, M. J., & Croninger, R. G. (2007). Sociocultural correlates of disciplinary exclusion among students with emotional, behavioral, and learning disabilities in the SEELS national dataset. *SAGE Journals*, 33–45. https://doi.org/10.1177/10634266070150010401

Albee, G. W. (1996). Revolutions and counterrevolutions in prevention. *American Psychologist*, 1130–1133.

American Juvenile Justice System. (2009). *In Wikipedia*. https://en.wikipedia.org/wiki/American_juvenile_justice_system

American Psychological Association Zero Tolerance Task Force. (2008). Are zero tolerance policies effective in the schools? An evidentiary review and recommendations. *American Psychological Association*, 1–141. https://doi.org/10.1037/0003-066X.63.9.852

Bahena, S., Cooc, N., Currie-Rubin, R., Kuttner, P., & Ng, M. (2012). Disrupting the school-to-prison pipeline. *Harvard Educational Review*.

Butts, J. A., & Travis, J. (2002). *The rise and fall of American youth violence*. The Urban Institute of Justice. www.urban.org/sites/default/files/publication/60381/410437-The-Rise-and-Fall-of-American-Youth-Violence.PDF60381

Carter, P. L. (2005). *Keepin' it real: School success beyond black and white*. Oxford University Press.

Catalano, R. F., Berglund, M. L., Ryan, J. A. M., Lonczak, H. S., & Hawkins, J. D. (2004). Positive youth development in the United States: Research findings on evaluations of positive youth development programs. *Annals of the American Academy of political and Social Sciences, 591*, 98–124.

Cokley, K., Cody, B., Smith, L., Beasley, S., Miller, I. S., Hurst, A., Olufunke, A., Stone, S., & Jackson, S. (2014, November 21). Bridge over troubled waters, meeting the mental health needs of black students. *Phi Delta Kappan, 96*, 40–45. https://doi.org/10.1177/0031721714561445

Development Services Group, Inc. (2018). *Interactions between youth and law enforcement. Literature review*. Office of Juvenile Justice and Delinquency Prevention. www.ojjdp.gov/mpg/litreviews/Interactions-Youth-Law-Enforcement.pdf

Engel, G. L. (1977, April 8). The need for a new medical model: A challenge for biomedicine. *Science, 196*(4286), 129–136. https://doi.org/10.1126/science.847460. PMID: 847460.

Gannon, M. (2016). Race is a social construct, scientists argue. *Scientific American*.

Goodrich, S. A., Anderson, S. A., & LaMotte, V. (2014). Evaluation of a program designed to promote positive police and youth interactions. *Journal of Juvenile Justice, 3*(2), 55.

Kupchik, A. (2012). *Homeroom security: School discipline in an age of fear.* NYU Press.

Lawrence, R., & Hemmens, C. (2008). *Juvenile justice: A text/reader.* Sage.

Mallett, C. A. (2016). *The school-to-prison pipeline, A comprehensive assessment.* Springer Publishing Company.

McCurdy, J. (2014). Targets for arrest. In A. J. Nocella II, P. Parmar, & D. Stovall (Eds.), *From education to incarceration: Dismantling the school-to-prison pipeline* (pp. 86–101). Peter Lang.

Models for Change. (2011). *Juvenile diversion guidebook.* Center for Juvenile Justice Reform, National Center for Mental Health and Juvenile Justice, National Juvenile Defender Center, National Youth Screening and Assessment Project, and Robert F. Kennedy Children's Action Corps

Myers, W. C., Burton, P. R., Sanders, P. D., Donat, K. M., Donat, Cheney, J., Fitzpatrick, T. M., & Monaco, L. (2000). Project back-on-track at 1 year: A delinquency treatment program for early-career juvenile offenders. *Journal of American Child and Adolescent Psychiatry, 39*(9), 1127–1134. https://doiorg/10.1097/00004583-200009000-00012

NAACP Legal Defense and Educational Fund. (n.d.). *Dismantling the school-to-prison pipeline.* file:///C:/Users/csrat/Desktop/Articles%20for%20School%20to%20prison%20pipeline/Dismantling_the_School_to_Prison_Pipeline__Criminal-Justice__.pdf

Nastasi, B. K., Varjas, K., & Bernstein, R. (1997). *Exemplary mental health programs: School psychologists as mental health service providers.* National Association of School Psychologists.

Nation, M., Crusto, C., Wandersman, A., Kumpfer, K., Seybolt, D., Morrissey-Kane, E., & Davino, K. (2003). What works in prevention: Principles of effective prevention programs. *American Psychologist, 58*(6–7), 449–456. https://doi.org/10.1037/0003-066X.58.6-7.449

The National Research Council and the Institute of Medicine. (2009). *Preventing mental, emotional, and behavioral disorders among young people: Progress and possibilities.* The National Academies Press. https://doi.org/10.17226/12480.

Rudd, T. (2014, February). *Racial disproportionality in school discipline: Implicit bias is heavily implicated.* Kirwan Institute Issue Brief. http://kirwaninstitute.osu.edu/wp-content/uploads/2014/02/racial-disproportionality-schools-02.pdf

Sandler, J. (2007). Community-based practices: Integrating dissemination theory with critical theories of power and justice. *American Journal of Community Psychology, 40*, 272–289.

Skiba, R. J., Horner, R. H., Chung, C., Rausch, M. K., May, S. L., & Tobin, T. (2011). Race is not neutral: A national investigation of African American and Latino disproportionality in school discipline. *School Psychology Review, 40*(1), 85–107.

Skiba, R. J., Michael, R. S., Nardo, A. C., & Peterson, R. (2002). The color of discipline: Sources of racial and gender disproportionality in school punishment. *The Urban Review, 34*(4), 317–342.

Snyder, H., & Sickmund, M. (1999). *Juvenile offenders and victims: 1999 report* (National Center for Juvenile Justice). Office of Juvenile Justice and Delinquency Prevention. https://ojjdp.ojp.gov/library/publications/juvenile-offenders-and-victims-1999-national-report

Teplin, L. A., Abram, K. M., Washburn, Welty, L. J., Hershfield, J. A., & Dulcan, M. K. (2013). *The Northwestern juvenile project: Overview.* Office of Juvenile Justice and Delinquency Prevention.

Thattai, D. V. (2017). *A history of public education in the United States editorial summary.* Research Gate.

U.S. Department of Education. (2022). *School climate and discipline: Know the data. Up to Date.* Retrieved January 22, 2022, from https://www2.ed.gov/p0licy/gen/gui/school-discipline/data.html

U.S. Department of Health and Human Services. (1999). *Mental health: A report of the surgeon general.* U. S. Department of Health and Human Services, Substance Abuse and Mental Health Services Administration, Center for Mental Health Services. *National Institutes of Health, National Institute of Mental Health*

U.S. Department of Housing and Urban Development. (2012). *Housing discrimination against racial and ethnic minorities 2012.* Office of Policy Development and Research. Retrieved January 31, 2022, from www.huduser.gov/portal/Publications/pdf/HUD-514_HDS2012.pdf

Vera, E. M., & Kenny, M. E. (2013). *Social justice and culturally relevant prevention.* SAGE. https://dx.doi.org/10.4135/9781452275598

Wald, J., & Kurlaender, M. (2003). Connected in Seattle? An exploratory study of student perceptions of discipline and attachments to teachers. In J. Wald & D. Losen (Eds.), *New directions for youth development* (pp. 35–54). Jossey-Bass. https://doi.org/10.1002/yd.53. PMID: 14635433.

Wald, J., & Losen, D. J. (2003). *New directions for youth development: Deconstructing the school-to-prison pipeline.* Jossey-Bass.

2

THE PRISON INDUSTRIAL COMPLEX

Between 1995 and 2019, juvenile justice agencies made enormous progress in the reduction of youth incarceration rates, bringing them down by as much as 70%. However, the rate of incarceration of all youth in the United States remains disturbingly higher than in any other industrialized country in the world (The Annie E. Casey Foundation, 2021). The most recent cross-national comparison of youth justice was conducted by Hazel in 2008, where 336 out of 100,000 youth under the age of 18 in the United States were in custody. As is seen in Figure 2.1, the next highest countries were South Africa, with 69 out of 100,000, and New Zealand, with 68 out of 100,000 youth in custody. In 2017, 43,580 youth were held in residential placements each night, another 935 were incarcerated in adult prisons, and an estimated 76,000 were prosecuted, sentenced, or incarcerated as adults in the United States.

Iatrogenic—A Cure That Makes Problems Worse

State juvenile corrections systems in the United States confine youth in many types of facilities, including group homes, residential treatment centers, boot camps, wilderness programs, and county-run youth facilities, but the largest share of committed youth are held in locked, long-term correctional facilities. These facilities are typically operated by state governments or private firms under contract and are operated in a

18

DOI: 10.4324/9781003284383-3

Unit	No. of Convicted under—18 in Prison (Incidence)	% of Prison Population under 18	Young People per 100K of Relevant Population
England & Wales**	2,869	3.8	46.8
Australia	545	2.4	24.9
Austria*	114	1.5	-
Belgium*	105	1.1	-
Bulgaria*	121	1.3	-
Croatia*	7	0.3	-
Denmark*	12	0.3	-
Finland**	7	0.2	3.6
France**	751	1.2	18.6
Germany	841	1.4	23.1
Italy**	267	0.5	11.3
Japan**	7	0.0	0.1
Netherlands**	574	3.1	51.3
New Zealand**	369	6.4	68.0
Norway*	13	0.5	-
Portugal*	289	2.1	-
Scotland**	170	2.6	33.0
South Africa**	4,158	2.2	69.0
Spain*	136	0.3	-
Sweden**	14	0.2	4.1
Turkey*	2,237	3.7	-
USA**	104,413	-	336.0

Figure 2.1 Cross-National Comparison of Youth Justice—Numbers of Under 18 in Custody

Note: Figure 2.1 collates figures cited in images and Dignan (2006) and Muncie (2006) on the number of young people aged less than 18 years in custody at any one time. Where the sources gave conflicting figures, the most recently compiled total has been selected. (*Figures for September 2002. Council of Europe, 2002, cited in Muncie, 2006. **Various collated figures from national statistics, Cavadino & Dignan, 2006.) From Cross-National Comparison of Youth Justice *by Neal Hazel, 2008, The University of Salford, Youth Justice Board*

regimented, prison-like fashion featuring correctional hardware, such as razor-wire, isolation cells, and locked cell blocks. These facilities, however, have not been found to reduce the criminality of troubled young people. In fact, available studies of youth released from residential corrections programs have found that 70–80% are rearrested within two or three years of release. Of those youth released from juvenile corrections facilities, 38–58% are found guilty of new offenses as juveniles or adults within two years, and 45–72% are found guilty within three years of release (Mendel, 2011).

Long-term cohort studies paint a similarly bleak picture of training schools' impact on future offending. One such study in New York State found that 89% of boys and 81% of girls released from state juvenile corrections institutions in the early 1990s were arrested as adults by age 28. Among boys, 65% were convicted of felonies by age 28, and 71% were incarcerated in an adult jail or prison, or what Golash-Boza (2019) and Selman and Leighton (2010) call the Prison Industrial Complex. In the publication *No Place for Kids*, Paul DeMuro, who served as commissioner of the Pennsylvania juvenile corrections system in the late 1970s and has since served as an expert witness in numerous legal cases concerning conditions of confinement in juvenile facilities, was quoted as saying, "The best way to describe America's addiction to training schools is 'iatrogenic'— a cure that makes problems worse" (Mendel, 2011, p. 4).

As is indicated in Chapter 1, African American youth are more likely to be detained and committed than any other racial group. In fact, African American youth are more than four times as likely to be detained or committed in juvenile facilities as their White peers, according to nationwide data collected in October 2019. During that time, the overall youth placement rate was 114 per 100,000. The African American youth rate, however, was 315 per 100,000, compared to the White youth placement rate of 72 per 100,000. Although African American youth comprised only 15% of all youth across the United States when these data were examined, they constituted 41% of youth in placement (The Sentencing Project, 2021).

According to Stevenson (2014), a public interest lawyer and executive director of the Equal Justice Initiative, on any given day in this country, 10,000 children are in adult jails and prisons where they face a five times greater rate of sexual violence and an eight times greater rate of suicide. No other country in the world imprisons its citizens as is done in the United States. In 1972, there were 300,000 people in jails and prisons. Today, there are 2.3 million. Of those behind bars, African Americans and others of African American descent make up about 40% of the inmates (2014).

Changing the Dysfunctional Narrative

One out of every 100 American adults is incarcerated, a per capita rate that is 5–10 times higher than that in Western Europe or other democracies. The United States has only 5% of the world's population, but it has nearly 25% of its prisoners. This difference between us and the rest of the developed world, Stevenson (2014) said, has less to do with an increase in violent crime and more to do with broader social and psychological dynamics in our society that need more attention at scientific and professional gatherings. One such dynamic is proximity. He wrote the following:

> We work with children and we talk about children, but we don't actually spend time with them. We talk about criminal justice reform and violence, but we don't get close to the people who are engaged in and experience these acts. We have allowed our distance from the needs of children and our failure to understand these dynamics to make us comfortable tolerating these realities.
>
> (p. 61)

Those working toward justice, Stevenson went on to say, need to focus on changing the dysfunctional narrative that has emerged about the mental health needs of people in the criminal justice system because that narrative is disconnected from what science tells us. Through working in very poor communities, Stevenson frequently sees children who have been traumatized by violence. It is impossible, however, for these children to conform to behavioral expectations if trauma is not seen as a disability. Most of these children live in violent communities, go to violent schools, and routinely see and experience acts of violence, but when they act violently, we call them violent offenders as if, somehow, they are the aberration. To change the narrative, he says, the word "trauma" needs to be applied more frequently. "If we don't use that word, we don't use all of the resources, skills and interventions we know and have that can help people suffering from trauma recover" (2014, p. 61). The staggering number of military men and women returning from war with post-traumatic stress disorder has recently made this mental health condition a household word. Americans are appalled when they hear that these individuals do not receive the mental health support they need and deserve or that their mental health condition has resulted in violence, such as suicide or homicide. In contrast, however, the efforts needed to prevent trauma from occurring in the lives of at-risk youth are frequently met with fierce debate, and similar sentiments are rarely given when these youths become violent.

Court-Level Practices

As is previously indicated, the overall body of recidivism evidence indicates that confinement in youth correctional facilities does not always work as a strategy to steer delinquent youth away from crime. In addition to recidivism analyses, criminologists have conducted more sophisticated studies to pinpoint the impact of juvenile confinement on the criminal careers of delinquent youth. The vast majority of studies found that incarceration is no more effective than probation or alternative sanctions in reducing the criminality of adjudicated youth, and incarceration is particularly ineffective for less-serious youthful offenders. In fact, many studies have found that incarceration actually increases recidivism among youth with lower-risk profiles and less-serious offending histories.

Of the nearly 150,000 delinquent youth placed into residential programs by juvenile courts for delinquency in 2007, only 12% were committed for serious crimes, such as murder, rape, robbery, and aggravated assault (Mendel, 2011). So, why are juvenile courts sending so many low-level offenders to correctional institutions? Research has revealed that some of these juvenile offenders enter correctional facilities because of questionable court-level practices. According to Mendel (2011), available evidence points to some of these factors:

> **Lack of Programs and Services**: Judges face considerable challenges in the placement of low-level youthful offenders, according to Whitman, former governor of New Jersey. For example, a judge in one county has many options to craft appropriate orders for young offenders, but in another county, especially if it is an urban county,

a judge may have very few options between probation and incarceration. These options are like choosing between an aspirin or a lobotomy for a migraine (as cited in Mendel, 2001). The options available to the courts for young, low-level offenders depend more on funding than on the seriousness of the offense. This, of course, is an unfortunate and potentially dangerous aspect of many juvenile court systems, especially for low-risk and less serious offenders.

Counterproductive Financial Incentives: Many local juvenile courts and probation agencies face strong financial incentives to place youth in state custody instead of providing community-based support because most states pay the full cost to incarcerate juveniles in state facilities. In the publication *No Place for Kids*, Mendel reported that of the 38 states where local courts or probation agencies oversee community supervision and treatment programs, substantial state funding is rarely provided (2011).

Dumping Grounds: In addition to schools, juvenile correctional systems have become the primary point of service for youth with mental health conditions and other serious disadvantages who could be more appropriately and effectively rehabilitated by other service agencies. This is, in part, a result of the collapse of public mental health services for children and adolescents. The closing of many and, in some states, all of the residential facilities for seriously disturbed youth during the 1990s resulted in juvenile justice becoming the primary referral for youth with mental disorders.

Punishment of Defiance, Not Delinquency: Many youths without serious offending histories are placed into custody for repeatedly violating rules and/or behaving disrespectfully toward judges, probation officers, and other people in authority. In a national study, nearly 12% of delinquent youth in secure correctional custody were incarcerated for violating probation or aftercare rules, not for committing new crimes (Mendel, 2011).

Abuse of the Court System: Some juveniles have also entered correctional facilities due to abuse of the court system. For example, in 2008, a scandal unfolded over judicial kickbacks at Luzerne County Court of Common Pleas in Wilkes-Barre, Pennsylvania. Two judges, Mark Ciavarella and Michael Conahan, were convicted of accepting money in return for imposing harsh sentences on juveniles to increase capacity at the PA Child Care for-profit detention centers. This became known as the "Kids for Cash" scandal (Kids for Cash Scandal, 2022).

The Costs and Consequences of Incarceration

The costs and consequences of incarcerating juveniles in correctional facilities are varied and in many cases temporal. These juveniles eventually become adults and many times become parents. Some of the most insidious costs adversely affect their families, the mental health of youth and adults for generations, and this country's economy.

Economic Costs: Although non-residential programming options deliver equal or better results for a fraction of the cost, most states still devote the bulk of their juvenile justice budgets to correctional institutions and other facility placements. In 2008, it cost an average of $241 per day ($66,000 to $88,000 per 9–12 months) to incarcerate a young person in a juvenile correctional facility. This sum is many times the average annual per-pupil expenditures for public elementary and secondary schools and far surpasses the costs of a public four-year university or two-year community/technical college. These fees are also excessive when compared to high-quality mentoring programs, such as Big Brothers/Big Sisters, which are slightly less than $1,000 per participant, and the YouthBuild career preparation program, which is $17,000 per participant (Mendel, 2011).

Costs to Children's Mental Health: As is indicated earlier, on any given day in this country, 10,000 children are in adult jails and prisons where they face a five times greater rate of trauma and an eight times greater rate of suicide (Stevenson, 2014). Three out of every 10 confined youth in correctional facilities have, on at least one occasion, attempted suicide (Teplin et al., 2013). The trauma of being separated from a parent can also multiply existing mental health issues, such as depression and anxiety, and hamper educational achievement (Wildeman, 2014). In magnitude, incarceration has been found to be the same as abuse, domestic violence, and divorce, with potentially lasting negative impacts on a child's well-being (Allard & Martin, 2016).

Having a parent incarcerated is another stressful and traumatic experience for children. It means the loss of a parent's support during critical early years when families and communities should be laying the foundation for healthy development and success. Bonds to that parent are also weakened or never formed, especially if the incarcerated parent is the mother (The Annie E. Casey Foundation, 2016). Kids of incarcerated mothers are also at greater risk of dropping out of school, and they are more likely to contend with poor mental and physical health upon reaching adulthood (Murphey & Cooper, 2015).

Temporal Costs: The temporal costs of incarceration are not as obvious as those that affect America's economy or the mental health of youth, largely because many occur over years and even generations. Because of this, temporal costs are insidious and become even more detrimental over time. As is indicated earlier in this chapter, many studies have found that incarceration increases recidivism among youth with lower-risk profiles and less-serious offending histories, and follow-up studies tracking youth released from residential corrections programs have found that 70–80% are rearrested within two or three years, some because of new offenses. It is somewhat ironic that teachers and other staff members in the public schools have been condemned by the general public, media, and state and federal politicians for poor achievement outcomes, while criticisms are rarely levied against the efficacy of the similarly funded training schools and prisons, which frequently produce iatrogenic results at horrendous and immeasurable individual and societal costs.

Over time, incarceration can devastate whole communities, particularly when men cannot provide for their families and are absent from their children. Their absence results in higher poverty rates and an increased likelihood of mental and behavioral health issues for members of the younger generation. Both of these factors can lead to incarceration and a perpetual cycle of imprisonment from one generation to the next. An overwhelming number of incarcerated parents are young fathers. In fact, about 45% of young fathers who are in state and federal prisons are age 24 or younger (La Vigne et al., 2008). Children with an incarcerated parent are typically younger than 10 years old, live in low-income African American families, and have a young, single mother who has limited education (Murphey & Cooper, 2015).

When parents spend time in prison, their children's health and health behaviors are affected for decades, the journal *Pediatrics* suggests. Researchers examined data on about 13,000 young adults (ages 24 to 32), of whom 10% had had a parent incarcerated during their childhood. These participants were more likely to forgo needed health care, smoke, abuse alcohol and illicit drugs, and engage in risky sexual behavior. These results held after controlling for factors such as gender, race, age, and parental education (Heard-Garris et al., 2018).

Even if parents were not living with their children before incarceration, more than half still provided the primary financial support (La Vigne et al., 2008). Children feel the absence of an adult, whether for several nights in jail or years in prison (Geller et al., 2012). They feel it when their refrigerator is bare because their family has lost an income source, when they must move (sometimes repeatedly) because their families can no longer afford the rent or mortgage, and when they hear whispers in school, at church, or in their neighborhood about where their mother or father has gone. Nationally, the percentage of children with an incarcerated parent varies from 3% in New Jersey to 13% in Kentucky, but the total number of kids who have had a parent in jail or prison at some point in their childhood hovers around 5.1 million, which is still a conservative estimate (The Annie E. Casey Foundation, 2016).

Families are the building blocks of communities and nations, and despite anyone's personal views about crime and punishment, most will agree that incarceration breaks up families. Consequently, kids with incarcerated parents are significantly less likely to live in neighborhoods that are supportive of families. Parents are also more likely to report feeling unsafe in these communities and less likely to feel they have people they can rely on for help. Communities most afflicted by high incarceration rates have high levels of poverty, unemployment, and racial segregation. These communities have been described by Burch (2013), a political scientist, as neighborhoods where African American and poor people live.

Nationally, people with criminal convictions also face serious challenges in finding stable and adequate employment to support their families, partly due to the strong stigma that can discourage potential employers. In some states, legal barriers prevent people with criminal convictions from holding certain jobs, and those who find employment typically earn less than otherwise similar individuals who have not been incarcerated. A Pew study found that men with a previous criminal conviction worked roughly nine fewer weeks and earned 40% less each year than otherwise similar non-offenders. In addition, this study found that incarceration reduces the total earnings of all African American men, not just ex-offenders, by 9% (Mitchell & Leachman, 2014). These costs to communities are frequently overlooked, but their impact is incalculable.

Collateral Consequences: A new term called "collateral consequences" has been introduced to describe the impact that incarceration has made on individuals', families', and children's mental health and wellbeing. Collateral consequences are criminal convictions that are not part of civil and state penalties. They are legal and regulatory sanctions and restrictions that limit or prohibit people with criminal records from accessing employment, occupational licensing, housing, voting, education, and other opportunities (Justice Center, 2016). One of the most disturbing contemporary implications of these consequences was made by Alexander (2012), an acclaimed civil rights lawyer, advocate, and legal scholar, through the publication of *The New Jim Crow*. In this book, Alexander argued that America is not an egalitarian democracy, but one that uses the criminal justice system to label African Americans as "criminals." Alexander went on to write that, in the age of colorblindness when it is no longer permissible to use race explicitly as a justification for discrimination, exclusion, and social contempt, the criminal justice system is used instead. This, she said, makes it perfectly legal to discriminate against African Americans in employment, housing, voting rights, educational opportunities, food stamps and other public benefits, and jury service, especially if they are labeled as felons.

Alexander's comments are reminiscent of a similar state of affairs described by Frederick Douglas over one-hundred years ago regarding the Convict Lease System and Lynch Law. These were racially repressive systems that flourished in many parts of the United States at the end of The American Civil War when farmers and businessmen in the South needed replacements for the labor force they had lost when their slaves were freed. The states began leasing convicts as laborers on plantations and other facilities, which provided cheap labor for the plantations and much-needed revenue for the states. Ninety percent of these convict laborers were African Americans, and it became a lucrative practice for states and counties to be quick to convict African Americans. Prison populations increased all over the South, especially in states such as Alabama, Arkansas, Florida, Georgia, Kentucky, Louisiana, Mississippi, Nebraska, North Carolina, South Carolina, Tennessee, and Washington, which claimed to be too poor to maintain state convicts within prison walls. Therefore, the convicts were leased out to work for railway contractors, mining companies, and those who farmed large plantations. These companies assumed charge of the convicts, worked them as cheap labor, and paid the states a handsome revenue.

Lynch Laws were not laws at all, but rather racial terrorism that was inflicted on African Americans by Whites to maintain the status quo. Although the Emancipation Proclamation was issued by President Abraham Lincoln on January 1, 1863, and declared all persons held as slaves to be free, the United States still sanctioned and promoted racial inequality by turning a blind eye toward the ways in which violence was used to enforce that inequality for over 100 years. There is considerable inconsistency in these numbers, largely because many lynching were never reported, but according to Rasmussen (2011), White Southerners lynched close to 4,000 African Americans between 1882 and 1965, and the American government did little, if anything, to prevent this violent enforcement of Jim Crow rule. In 1893, Frederick Douglas described the Convict Lease System and Lynch Law as the twin infamies under which people of color suffer.

It would be wonderful to conclude that the conditions Douglas described over one hundred years ago did not have any relevance to today, especially since the Convict Lease System ended in 1928 (Fierce, 1994) and the Civil Rights Movement all but ended lynching in the 1960s. Other forms of convict labor, however, continued in various forms for decades (Sellin, 1976). These other systems included plantations, industrial prisons, and chain gangs. Peonage, a form of involuntary servitude that relies on debt to compel the worker, was also a problem for poor African Americans who became entrapped by systems of low pay and indebtedness to company or plantation stores. While we no longer see peonage in exactly that form today, many African Americans remain trapped by a bondage of a different sort. The exponential increase in incarcerations of African Americans over the past forty years has resulted in higher poverty rates, an increased likelihood of mental and behavioral health issues for members of the younger generation, and a lack of family support. These factors also increase the chances of a child entering the school-to-prison pipeline, which could result in a perpetual cycle of imprisonment for generations.

References

Alexander, M. (2012). *The new Jim Crow*. The New Press.

Allard, P., & Martin, G. E. (2016, June 20). #BlackDadsMatter: Mass incarceration is robbing children of their fathers. Here's how to fix that. *Justice Strategies*. www.justicestrategies.org/coip/blog/2016/06/blackdadsmatter-mass-incarceration-robbing-children-their-fathers-heres-how-fix-it

The Annie E. Casey Foundation. (2016, April 19). *Children of incarcerated parents, a shared sentence*. https://assets.aecf.org/m/resourcedoc/aecf-asharedsentence-2016.pdf

The Annie E. Casey Foundation. (2021, July). *Youth residing in juvenile detention, correctional and/or residential facilities in the United States*. Retrieved July 31, 2021, from https://datacenter.kidscount.org/data/tables/42-youth-residing-in-juvenile-detention-correctional-and-or-residential-facilities#detailed/1/any/false/1729,871,573,36,867,133,18,17,14,12/any/319,17599

Burch, T. (2013). *Trading democracy for justice*. University of Chicago Press. https://press.uchicago.edu/ucp/books/book/chicago/T/bo16382

Cavadino, M., & Dignan, P. (2006). *Penal systems: A comparative approach*. Sage.

Douglas, F. (1893). *Convict lease system, Frederick Douglass papers*. https://picryl.com/media/convict-lease-system-81322f

Fierce, M. (1994). *Slavery revisited: Blacks and the southern convict lease system, 1865–1933*. Africana Studies Center Brooklyn.

Geller, A., Cooper, C., Garfinkel, I., Schwartz-Soicher, O., & Mincy, R. (2012). Father incarceration and child development. *Demography*, 49–76.

Golash-Boza, T. M. (2019). *Race and racisms*. Oxford University Press.

Hazel, N. (2008). *Cross-national comparison of youth justice*. Youth Justice Board. www.youthpolicy.org/library/documents/cross-national-comparison-of-youth-justice/

Heard-Garris, N., Winkelman, T. N. A., Choi, H., Miller, A. K., Kan, K., Shlafer, R., & Davis, M. M. (2018, September 1). Health care use and health behaviors among young adults with history of parental incarceration. *Pediatrics*. https://publications.aap.org/pediatrics/article/142/3/e20174314/38619/Health-Care-Use-and-Health-Behaviors-Among-Young?autologincheck=redirected

Justice Center. (2016). *Collateral consequences*. niccc.csgjusticecenter.org

Kids for Cash Scandal. (2022, February 5). *In Wikipedia*. https://en.wikipedia.org/wiki/Kids_for_cash_scandal

La Vigne, N. G., Davies, E., & Brazzell, D. (2008, February). *Broken bonds: Understanding and addressing the needs of children with incarcerated parents*. U. S. Department of Justice. www.ojp.gov/ncjrs/virtual-library/abstracts/broken-bonds-understanding-and-addressing-needs-children

Mendel, R. A. (2001). *Less cost, more safety: Guiding lights for reform in juvenile justice.* American Youth Policy Forum. https://www.ojp.gov/ncjrs/virtual-library/abstracts/less-cost-more-safety-guiding-lights-reform-juvenile-justice#additional-details-0

Mendel, R. A. (2011). *No place for kids.* The Annie E. Casey Foundation. https://assets.aecf.org/m/resourcedoc/aecf-NoPlaceForKidsFullReport-2011.pdf

Mitchell, M., & Leachman, M. (2014, October 28). *Changing priorities: State criminal justice reforms and investments in education.* Center for Budget and Policy Priorities.

Muncie, J. (2006, February). Repenalisation and rights: Explorations in comparative youth criminology. *The Howard Journal of Criminal Justice, 45*(1), 42.

Murphey, D., & Cooper, P. M. (2015, October). *Parents behind bars: What happens to their children?* Child Trends. www.childtrends.org/wp-content/uploads/2015/10/2015-42ParentsBehindBars.pdf

Rasmussen, D. (2011). *American uprising: The untold story of America's largest slave revolt.* HarperCollins Publishers.

Sellin, T. (1976). *Slavery and the penal system.* Elsevier.

Selman, D., & Leighton, P. (2010). *Punishment for sale: Private prisons, big business, and the incarceration binge.* Rowman & Littlefield Publishers, Inc.

The Sentencing Project. (2021, July). *Black disparities in youth incarceration.* www.sentencingproject.org/publications/black-disparities-youth-incarceration/

Stevenson, B. (2014). Want justice? *Monitor,* 61.

Teplin, L. A., Abram, K. M., Washburn, J. J., Welty, L. J., Hershfield, J. A., & Dulcan, M. K. (2013). *The Northwestern juvenile project: Overview.* Office of Justice Programs, Office of Juvenile Justice and Delinquency Prevention. https://ojjdp.ojp.gov/sites/g/files/xyckuh176/files/pubs/234522.pdf

Wildeman, C. (2014). Parental incarceration, child homelessness, and the invisible consequences of mass imprisonment. *The Annals of the American Academy of Political and Social Science,* 74–96

SECTION II
HOW ADVERSE PRACTICES "FUEL" THE PIPELINE

3

ADVERSE SCHOOL-LEVEL PRACTICES

Chapters 1 and 2 explain what the school-to-prison pipeline (STPP) is, explore its long-term history, and examine the United States' unique position as a free country that confines more youth than any industrialized country in the world. This chapter examines how adverse practices in schools, such as declining school funding (which includes funding equity and funding variations), resegregation of schools by race and class, zero tolerance disciplinary policies, and the increased utilization and federal funding of police officers in schools, increase the chances of a child entering the STPP.

Declining School Funding

It has been argued that the STPP begins for most students as a result of inadequate public school resources, equating to overcrowded classrooms, a lack of qualified teachers, and insufficient funding for "extras" such as counselors, special education services, and even textbooks. In an article written by Brown (2016) from The Washington Post, it was revealed that the nation's per-pupil spending on K–12 public schools had climbed steadily by at least 1% per year from 1996 to 2008 but hit a plateau and fell more than 1% in 2011, continuing into 2013 and reversing more than a decade of funding increases. Spending varies widely across the country, from a low $5,539 per student in Utah's Alpine School District to $20,331 in New York City, with a national average in 2013 of $10,763. Some states have also cut income tax rates, weakening their main revenue sources for supporting schools. For example, in 2015, the latest year for which comprehensive spending data are available from the U.S. Census Bureau, 29 states were still providing less total school funding per student than they were in 2008 (Leachman et al., 2017). Factors such as these "lock" students into second-rate educational environments, which increases disengagement, dropouts, and the risk of later court involvement. In contrast, however, between 1986 and 2013, state corrections spending jumped 141% after adjusting for inflation. In terms of actual dollars, this is an increase from about $20 billion to over $47 billion (Mitchell, 2015).

Funding Equity

Equity in funding from one school district to another adds a new element of complexity to the school funding issue. Prior to 1965, most school districts were independently operated and financed by local governments and initiatives. With the passage of the Elementary and Secondary Education Act in 1965, federal monies were funneled to local school districts. As a result, public school funding in the United States now comes from federal, state, and local sources. Local revenue, such as property taxes, pays for nearly half of the funding of public schools. This is problematic because it creates large differences in funding between wealthy and impoverished communities (Leachman et al., 2017). These differences exist among states, school districts within each state, and even among schools within specific districts. Funding differences in the United States generate huge disparities in the quality of school buildings, facilities, curriculum, equipment for instruction, teacher experience and qualifications, class sizes, the presence of auxiliary professionals, and other resources. The US is the only developed nation that tolerates such disparities. Elsewhere in the developed world, public schools normally receive equal funding in rich and poor communities alike on the basis of the number of students enrolled (Biddle & Berliner, 2002).

Slavin (1999), an American psychologist who studies educational and academic issues, indicated that the principal reason districts within states often differ markedly in per-pupil expenditures is that school funding is almost always tied to property taxes, which is a direct function of local wealth. When school funding depends on local wealth, this creates a situation in which poor districts must tax themselves far more heavily than wealthy ones, yet they still may not be able to generate adequate income. He said that, to his knowledge, the US is the only nation to fund elementary and secondary education based on local wealth. Other developed countries either equalize funding or provide extra funding for individuals or groups they believe need it.

Resistance to equitable funding for all schools and all students has been supported by several belief systems about the causes of poverty. One of these is the ideology of individualism, which holds that success and failure result mainly from individual effort rather than social circumstances. People in the United States are known around the world for their strong belief in the power of personal effort, but this thought process can lead to associated beliefs that blame impoverished persons for their lack of success in life (Kluegel & Smith, 1986). Another belief system is essentialism, which attributes poverty to inherent genetic characteristics. When applied to the poor and minorities, essentialism asserts that poverty results from genetic flaws. Advocates of such a belief system have included psychologists Arthur Jensen (1972) and Richard Herrnstein (Herrnstein & Murray, 1994). A third belief system, the culture of poverty thesis, argues that many poor children fall behind because of inappropriate traditions in the subcultures of their homes, communities, or ethnic groups (Moynihan, 1969). Voicing these opinions openly is not always acceptable in the United States, and several studies published over the years in support of individualism and essentialism have since been found to be badly flawed. However, beliefs that justify all three ideologies are still embraced privately by many people who use them to rationalize resistance to proposals for equal school funding (Biddle & Berliner, 2002).

In contrast, data collected from strong studies by researchers such as Biddle (1997) and Elliott (1998) reported that funding levels are tied to sizable net effects for student outcomes. The joint results of school funding and student advantage are sizable, and achievement scores from United States school districts with substantial funding and low student poverty are similar to those earned by the highest-scoring countries in international comparative studies. For example, in a study that examined the effects generated by differences in school funding and student disadvantage among U.S. schools, the sizes of those effects were compared with disparities in achievement among different countries found in international comparisons. Data from the *Third International Mathematics and Science Study* (Mullins et al., 2001) compared 8th grade mathematics achievement scores of students in other nations with those of students in specific states, school districts, and school consortia within the United States. The two best-scoring entities in the United States were the Naperville Illinois Public School District and the "First-in-the-World" Consortium, which was composed of school districts from the Chicago North Shore area. Both of these entities were noted for having high levels of funding and serving low numbers of impoverished students. Both earned high achievement scores comparable to those of Hong Kong, Japan, and other top-scoring countries. The two worst-scoring U.S. entities at the time were Miami-Dade County Public Schools in Florida and the Rochester School District in New York. Both received low levels of funding and served many poor students, and each earned low achievement scores similar to Turkey, Jordan, and Iran, the worst-scoring nations in the study. It was concluded that differences in student advantage and funding in the United States generate achievement disparities that are comparable to those separating the highest- and lowest-achieving nations in international studies (Biddle & Berliner, 2002).

Overall, better-funded schools attract teachers with higher levels of education, more experience, and higher scores on competency tests, all of which appear to generate better achievement scores among students (Darling-Hammond & Post, 2000). Attracting teachers with higher levels of education, more experience, and higher scores on competency tests, however, is a major challenge for poor school districts that compete each year with affluent school districts that are also seeking the best teachers from a dwindling workforce. According to a new study by Sutcher et al. (2016) of The Learning Policy Institute (2016), teacher demand is on the rise as a function of changes in student enrollment, shifts in pupil-teacher ratios, and high levels of teacher attrition. Unfortunately, the supply of teachers is atypically low and has been declining. High levels of attrition hovering near 8% over the last decade are responsible for the largest share of the annual decline. This rate is much higher for beginning teachers and for those who work in high poverty and minority schools and districts. In addition, fewer college-bound students are entering college with the goal of becoming teachers. Between 2009 and 2014, the most recent data available, teacher education enrollments dropped from 691,000 to 451,000. To address this shortage, several states have greatly expanded emergency permits to allow the hiring of untrained teachers to meet their demands. As a result, during the 2013–14 school year, high-minority schools across the nation averaged four times as many uncertified teachers. This is a primary example of how, when there are not enough teachers to go around, schools with the fewest resources and the least desirable working conditions are often the most disproportionately impacted (Sutcher et al., 2016).

In addition to declining school funding and equity in funding, there is variation in funding within each school system. Although often ignored, school systems are some of the largest business entities in the United States. They are typically controlled at various levels by multiple sources, such as federal and state governments, county, or parish (such as in Louisiana) school systems, and local school boards, school superintendents, and principals within each school. How funding is prioritized by these sources is beyond the scope of this publication, but Rankin (2016) examined public records for the nation's ten largest school districts to uncover the ratio of counselors to security personnel. What she found is that of the largest five districts, three have more officers than counselors. Interestingly, each of these school districts counts students of color as the majority. These districts are New York City, Chicago, and Miami-Dade.

As is indicated earlier, the school-to-prison pipeline (STPP) begins for most students as a result of inadequate public school resources, equating to overcrowded classrooms, a lack of qualified teachers, and insufficient funding for "extras" such as counselors, special education services, and even textbooks. These inadequacies are largely the result of inadequate and inequitable school funding and, to some extent, how these funds are prioritized by each school system.

Racism and Resegregation of Schools by Race and Class

Another adverse nationwide school-level practice that can steer school-aged children into the STPP is the resegregation of schools by race and class. Although it has been over 60 years since the landmark case, Brown v. Board of Education (1954), at which time the U.S. Supreme Court unanimously ruled that American state laws establishing racial segregation in public schools are unconstitutional, contentious educational issues that are influenced by race and racism continue in the United States. According to Myers (as cited in Haggert, 2022), the concept of race was created to serve as the elusive justification for assigning value and allocating opportunity based on phenotypic differences, such as skin color, effectively privileging Whites and disenfranchising African Americans. Despite prevailing evidence that race is a social construct (Gannon, 2016) with no scientific merit, its impact on the United States is palpable.

Over the past few decades, genetic sequencing research has provided scientific support that all humans are closely related with the same collection of genes (with the exception of identical twins), but everyone has slightly different versions of some of them. The scientific fact is that our species, Homo sapiens, evolved in Africa (Kolbert, 2018). The recent rash of genetic testing certainly has complicated this issue, since many individuals assume that the few hundred years these test results cover provide a full picture of their genotype (their complete set of genetic material) and phenotype (their observable characteristics). However, analyses of mitochondrial DNA, which is passed down intact from mothers to daughters, indicate that all Homo sapiens on earth are descendants of a woman (popularly known as "Mitochondrial Eve") who lived in East Africa about 200,000 years ago (Cann et al., 1987). The first Homo sapiens left Africa about 100,000 years ago, migrated into the Middle East, and from there migrated to Asia. They did not enter Europe until about 35,000 years ago or the Americas until 15,000 to 20,000 years ago, when the oceans were much lower and Asia and Alaska were connected (Stringer, 2012). What we now call race is the product of genetic changes resulting from random mutations or tiny tweaks to DNA, the code of life. Mutations occur in humans, as in all species, at a fairly constant rate, so the longer a group persists, handing down its genes generation after generation, the more tweaks these genes will accumulate. Additionally, the longer two groups are separated, the more distinctive tweaks they will acquire (Kolbert, 2018).

As is indicated in Chapter 1, federal classifications recognize four races: African Americans (Blacks), American Indians and Alaska Natives, Asian Americans and Pacific Islanders, and White Americans (U. S. Office of Management and Budget, 1978). Unfortunately, these distinctions, along with suggested weaknesses, were partially based on the ideas promoted by Samuel Morton, a prominent 19th-century American scientist. Morton believed that people could be divided into five races based on the volume of the braincase. Morton claimed that Whites were the most intelligent of the races, East Asians were a step down, followed by Southeast Asians and Native Americans. African Americans were at the bottom. These ideas were quickly used, particularly in the South, by defenders of slavery. Today Morton is known as the father of scientific racism, and many of the horrors of the past few centuries can be traced to his idea that one race is inferior to another (Kolbert, 2018). Even in the 21st century, many of these beliefs persist and have allotted many White individuals throughout this country unearned status, privilege, and opportunity. Our current understanding of the term *White Privilege*, which originated from an article written by Peggy McIntosh (1989), addresses this phenomenon.

Current scientific evidence reveals that there is only one race: the human race. Vehement arguments fueled by race and racism continue and are frequently related to desegregation, school choice, and funding disparities, but unequivocal scientific evidence confirms the benefits of an integrated educational environment. Studies about the level of racial segregation in schools, for example, were found to have important implications for the educational outcomes of minority students. The desegregation efforts of the 1970s and 1980s led to substantial academic gains for African American students. The high school dropout rate also declined, and improved outcomes were seen in areas such as earnings, health, and incarceration. Unfortunately, many African American students continue to be concentrated in high-poverty, low-achieving schools, while White students are more likely to attend high-achieving, more affluent schools (Fiel, 2013).

In an article written by Kolbert (2018) for *National Geographic*, she said that, to an uncomfortable degree, we still live with Morton's legacy. His racial distinctions continue to shape our politics, our neighborhoods, and our sense of self. It was initially thought that school choice, such as charter and private schools, could potentially increase integration by drawing students from larger and more geographically diverse areas (as opposed to segregated neighborhoods), but this has not been consistently found to be the case. Studies conducted on the relationship between expanded school choice and school segregation show that, when these studies compare the racial composition of charter schools to local public schools, researchers typically find that charter schools preserve or intensify existing racial and economic segregation and/or facilitate white flight from public schools. Private schools, a second important type of school choice, don't fare any better than charter schools in integrating schools. During the 1970s, enrollment of Whites in these schools increased sharply, remained unchanged in the 1980s, and increased again in the 1990s. In a 2002 study, it was found that private schools continued to contribute to the persistence of school segregation in the south over the course of the 1990s (Reardon & Yun, 2003).

Magnet schools, another school option, were initially presented as an alternative to unpopular busing policies but included explicit desegregation goals along with provisions for recruiting and providing transportation for diverse populations. Although today's magnet schools are no longer as explicitly oriented toward integration efforts, in contrast to charter and private schools, they generally foster integration rather than hinder it (Frankenberg, & Siegel-Hawley (2009).

According to the report, *You Can't Fix What You Don't Look At: Acknowledging Race in Addressing Racial Discipline Disparities*, written by Carter et al. (2014), who were a part of The Discipline Disparities Research to Practice Collaborative (a group of 26 nationally known researchers, educators, advocates, and policy analysts), several poignant conclusions regarding the end of the legal sanctions upholding segregation were made. In this report, they said that physical separation across schools and districts by race and class remains the norm, and the structure of relationships between groups in our society remains largely segregated. This lessens the opportunity not only for students from historically disadvantaged backgrounds to have the same access to high-quality schools, but also for groups to interact and have their stereotypes of one another changed. Our experiences in schools are not just segregated physically but also socially and psychologically, which creates very real boundaries in lived experiences that make us unable to learn from and understand each other.

Segregation compounds economic inequality, with wealthier and predominantly White students in schools or classes with more opportunity and less-wealthy students of color in under-resourced and understaffed schools. There has not yet been a real and functional integration in school and society where we live together as equals. This has left us as a nation unable to learn from one another, surmount old stereotypes, and communicate and act effectively on the eradication of inequalities that run rampant in our schools and society. Despite the rapidly increasing diversity in our nation's student population, the majority of U.S. teachers remain female, White, and middle class, creating a within-school boundary in itself. In addition, many college students in pre-service education programs enter with little previous contact with racial groups other than their own, with pervasive negative stereotypes of other races that they can carry with them into schools and classrooms (Carter et al., 2014).

White teachers are not the only bearers of stereotypes. Middle-class, African American teachers are no less likely to evaluate students subjectively than their White, middle-class counterparts, which points to the complex dynamics of race and class. Sixty years after Brown v. the Board of Education, we remain surprisingly segregated as a society, and the benefits foreseen by integration, such as increased contact leading to the gradual fading of bias and stereotypes, have occurred less than expected. The challenges of pervasive stereotypes and vastly separate experiences for students and teachers of different races make it extremely difficult to come together as a society and honestly talk about the racial and ethnic stereotypes and inequalities that still afflict our schools and society and shape our school discipline patterns. These stereotypes, vastly separate experiences, and the widespread tendency to avoid the charged topic of race whenever possible provide few opportunities to reach out across those lines of social division and examine the causes of deep-seated inequalities in education in the United States, including disparities in suspension, expulsion, and school arrest (Carter et al., 2014). These experiences, or lack thereof, limit objectivity and fairness when African American students' behaviors are examined and discipline options are considered by teachers and administrators. They also provide few opportunities and insights that are needed for substantial changes in teachers' and administrators' perceptions, since it is indeed difficult to fix what you don't look at.

Zero Tolerance Disciplinary Policies

Another contentious issue that is inextricably linked to the STPP is zero tolerance policies and procedures. Since the early 1990s, school discipline has been dominated by the philosophy of zero tolerance. This philosophy was originally developed as an approach to drug enforcement, but the term became widely adopted in schools in the early 1990s as a philosophy or policy that mandates the application of predetermined consequences. Zero tolerance policies and procedures assume that removing students who engage in disruptive behavior will deter others from disruption and create an improved climate for those students who remain. Most often, these consequences are severe and punitive in nature, and they are intended to be applied regardless of the gravity of behavior, mitigating circumstances, or situational context (Skiba et al., 2006). No one can question the importance of maintaining a safe and disciplined learning environment, but as is indicated in previous chapters, recent data show significant disparities in the application of suspension and expulsion of students based on race (Kelley et al., 2021), which is where many students enter the STPP. In a recent study conducted by Del Toro and Wang (2021), these "grossly overrepresented" rates of school suspensions for minor disciplinary infractions were shown to also have a negative long-term effect on these students' grades.

Despite its 20-year history of implementation, there are few data that directly test the assumptions of a zero tolerance approach to school discipline. One of the most comprehensive studies of this approach was done by the American Psychological Association in 2006 (Skiba et al.). As part of its mission to advance health, education, and human welfare, the American Psychological Association (APA) commissioned the Zero Tolerance Task Force to examine evidence concerning the academic and behavioral effects of zero tolerance policies. The task force examined the assumptions that underlie zero tolerance policies and all data relevant to testing those assumptions in practice. It also synthesized the evidence regarding the specific effects of exclusionary discipline on students of color. The reader is encouraged to read the entire document by the APA for a complete review of this report, but in response to specific questions that are related to safety, discipline, race, and juvenile justice disciplinary alternatives, the following findings were revealed from this task force's extensive literature review.

1. Zero tolerance policies do not make schools safer or more effective in handling disciplinary issues. In terms of violence in schools, this task force indicated that the evidence does not support the assumption that violence in schools is out of control or increasing. According to their research, incidents of critical and deadly violence remain a relatively small proportion of school disruptions, and the data have consistently indicated that school violence and disruption have remained stable or have decreased since approximately 1985.

2. There was no evidence that zero tolerance has increased the consistency of school discipline. Rates of suspension and expulsion were found to vary widely across schools and school districts. In addition, this variation in suspension and expulsion appears to be due as much to characteristics of schools and school personnel (e.g., disciplinary philosophy, quality of school governance) as to the behavior or attitudes of students.

3. The impact of zero tolerance has had an adverse effect on students of color. As previously indicated, the appeal of zero tolerance policies is the expectation that by removing subjective influences or contextual factors from disciplinary decisions, such policies would be fairer to students traditionally overrepresented in school disciplinary consequences. The evidence did not support this assumption. Instead, the disproportionate discipline of students of color continues to be a concern. Overrepresentations

in suspension and expulsion were consistently found for African American students. This study also refuted the assumption that African American students exhibit higher rates of disruption or violence that would warrant higher rates of discipline. Rather, this task force hypothesized that African American students may be disciplined more severely for less serious or more subjective reasons due to the lack of teacher preparation in classroom management and training in culturally competent practices, and/or racial stereotypes.

4. Zero tolerance affects the relationship between education and the juvenile justice system. This task force concluded that the introduction of zero tolerance policies has affected the "delicate balance" between the educational and juvenile justice systems by increasing schools' use of and reliance on strategies such as security technology, security personnel, and profiling. This was found to be most prevalent in high-minority, high-poverty school districts. Additionally, it was found that the increased reliance on more severe consequences in response to student disruption has resulted in increased referrals to the juvenile justice system for infractions that were once handled in school.

This study concluded that other disciplinary alternatives could make a stronger contribution toward maintaining school safety and the integrity of the learning environment while keeping a greater number of students in school. These disciplinary alternatives include the following three levels of intervention:

- Primary prevention strategies targeted at all students,
- Secondary prevention strategies targeted at those students who may be at risk for violence or disruption, and
- Tertiary strategies targeted at those students who have already engaged in disruptive or violent behavior.

Comprehensive systems change models that use evidence-based interventions, such as schoolwide positive behavior interventions and supports (SWPBIS), restorative practices, Response to Intervention

(RTI), trauma-informed practices, and social-emotional learning, have also yielded promising results in terms of reduction in office referrals, school suspensions, and expulsions, as well as improved ratings on measures of school climate (Skiba et al., 2006).

School-level practices, such as zero tolerance disciplinary policies, are often considered the first step in a child's journey through the school-to-prison pipeline. According to the American Civil Liberties Union (ACLU), students of color and students with disabilities tend to be most affected because of an overreliance on discriminatory punitive school discipline policies, a lack of resources and training within schools, and ignorance regarding disability behaviors. The increased use of zero tolerance policies and other exclusionary practices, the ACLU says, like suspensions, expulsions, and referrals to law enforcement, decrease academic achievement and increase the likelihood that students will end up in jail cells rather than in college classrooms. In many schools that employ zero tolerance policies, minor misbehavior is criminalized, and police are called in to handle problems that should be managed by teachers or administrators, impacting these students' immediate lives and also their futures by increasing the likelihood that they will drop out and/or experience future criminal justice involvement (ACLU, 2012).

Increased Utilization and Federal Funding of Police Officers in Schools

Another adverse school-level practice has been the exponential use of police in schools. In 1975, principals in only 1% of the nation's schools reported police stationed in their buildings. By 1997, principals in 22% of all schools reported having a police officer stationed at least 1 hour per week or available as needed (Heaviside et al., 1998). By the 2003–2004 school year, 36% of principals reported police stationed in the schools, and by 2007–2008, the percentage had risen to 40%. According to Na and Gottfredson, the increased use of police in schools was driven in part by increased federal funding. The Department of Justice Office of Community Policing Services (COPS) initiated the "COPS in Schools" (CIS) grant program in 1999, just after the highly publicized shootings at Columbine High School. As of July 2005, COPS was awarded in excess of $753 million to more than 3,000 grantees to hire more than 6,500

school resource officers (SROs) through the CIS program and more than
$10 million to hire approximately 100 SROs through the Safe Schools/
Healthy Students program (2011).

As is indicated in the previous section, with growing frequency, many
school districts have begun relying on police rather than teachers and
administrators to maintain discipline. This practice impacts the lives of
students and also their futures by increasing the likelihood that they will
drop out of school and/or experience future criminal justice involvement.
As a result, children are far more likely to be subjected to school-based
arrests, a majority of which are for nonviolent offenses, than they were a
generation ago. The reliance on police in public schools has blurred the
lines between disciplining under a school's general policy standards and
disciplining according to law enforcement standards (ACLU, 2012).

References

American Civil Liberties Union. (2012). *Ending the school-to-prison pipeline*. www.aclu.
    org/sites/default/files/field_document/aclu_statement_for_sjc_subcomm_hearing_
    on_the_school_to_prison_pipeline_12_2012.pdf
Biddle, B. J. (1997). Foolishness, dangerous nonsense, and real correlates of state differ-
    ences in achievement. *Phi Delta Kappan*, *79*(1), 8–13.
Biddle, B. J., & Berliner, D. C. (2002). A research synthesis/unequal school funding in
    the United States. *Educational Leadership*, *59*(8), 48–59. https://eric.ed.gov/?q=
    EJ644983&id=EJ644983
Brown, E. (2016, January 27). Spending in nation's schools falls again, with wide varia-
    tions across states. *The Washington Post*.
Brown v. Board of Education, 347 U.S. 483 (1954). www.oyez.org/cases/1940-1955/
    347us483
Cann, R. L., Stoneking, M., & Wilson, A. C. (1987). Mitochondrial DNA and human
    evolution. *Nature*, 31–36.
Carter, P., Skiba, R., Arredondo, M., & Pollock, M. (2014). *You can't fix what you don't look
    at: Acknowledging race in addressing racial discipline disparities*. The Equity Project at
    Indiana University.
Darling-Hammond, L., & Post, L. (2000). Inequality in teaching and schooling: Sup-
    porting high-quality teaching and leadership in low-income schools. In R. D.
    Kahlenberg (Ed.), *A nation at risk: Preserving public education as an engine for social
    mobility* (pp. 127–167). The Century Foundation Press.
Elliott, M. (1998). School finance and opportunity to learn: Does money well spent
    enhance students' achievement? *Sociology of Education*, *71*(3), 223–245.
Fiel, J. E. (2013). Decomposing school resegregation: Social closure, racial imbalance, and
    racial isolation. *American Sociological Review*, *78*(5) 828–848. http://asr.sagepub.com
Frankenberg, E., & Siegel-Hawley, G. (2009). *Equity overlooked: Charter schools and
    civil rights policy*. The Civil Rights Project. University of California. https://
    civilrightsproject.ucla.edu/research/k-12-education/integration-and-diversity/equi
    ty-overlooked-charter-schools-and-civil-rights-policy/frankenberg-equity-over
    looked-report-2009.pdf

Gannon, M. (2016). Race is a social construct, scientists argue. *Scientific American*.

Haggert, M. (2022, March). Optimal psychology to address inequity: 4 Questions for Linda James Myers. *Monitor on Psychology*. https://www.apa.org/monitor/2022/03/conversation-myers

Heaviside, S., Rowand, C., Williams, C., & Farris, E. (1998). *Violence and discipline problems in U.S. public schools: 1996–97*. U.S. Department of Education, National Center for Education Statistics.

Herrnstein, R. J., & Murray, C. (1994). *The bell curve: The reshaping of American life by differences in intelligence*. The Free Press

Jensen, A. R. (1972). *Genetics and education*. Harper & Row

Kelley, B., Jamieson, C., & Perez Jr., Z. (2021, May 17). *50-state comparison: School discipline policies*. Education Commission of the States. www.ecs.org/50-state-comparison-school-discipline-policies/

Kluegel, J. R., & Smith, E. R. (1986). *Beliefs about inequality: American' view of what is and what ought to be*. Aldine de Gruyter.

Kolbert, E. (2018, October 22). There's no scientific basis for race—it's a made-up label. *National Geographic*. www.nationalgeographic.co.uk/people-and-culture/2018/04/theres-no-scientific-basis-race-its-made-label.

Leachman, M., Masterson, K., & Figueroa, E. (2017, November 29). *Center on budget and policy priorities*. www.cbpp.org/sites/default/files/atoms/files/11-29-17sfp.pdf

McIntosh, P. (1989, July/August). White privilege: Unpacking the invisible knapsack. *Peace and Freedom*. https://psychology.umbc.edu/files/2016/10/White-Privilege_McIntosh-1989.pdf

Mitchell, M. (2015, July 16). *States' high prison spending leaves less for classrooms*. Center on Budget and Policy Priorities. www.cbpp.org/blog/states-high-prison-spending-leaves-less-for-classrooms

Moynihan, D. P. (Ed.). (1969). *On understanding poverty: Perspectives from the social sciences*. Basic Books.

Mullins, I., Martin, M., Gonzalez, O'Connor, K., Chrostowski, S., Gregory, K., Garden, R., & Smith, T. (2001). *Mathematics benchmarking report: TIMSS 1999-Eighth grade achievement for U.S. states and districts in an international context*. Boston College

Na, C., & Gottfredson, D. C. (2011, October 11). Police officers in schools: Effects on school crime and the processing of offending behaviors. *Justice Quarterly, 30*, 619–650. https://doi.org/10.1080/07418825.2011.615754

Rankin, K. (2016, March 29). Study: Nation's largest public schools have more police than counselors. *COLORLINES*. www.colorlines.com/articles/study-nations-largest-public schools-have-more-police-counselors

Reardon, S. F., & Yun, J. T. (2003). Integrating neighborhoods, segregating schools: The retreat from school desegregation in the South, 1990–2000 (PDF). *North Carolina Law Review*, 81. https://scholarship.law.unc.edu/nclr/vol81/iss4/5

Skiba, R., Reynolds, C. R., Graham, S., Sheras, P., Conoley, J. C., & Garcia-Vazquez, E. (2006). *Are zero tolerance policies effective in the schools? An evidentiary review and recommendations*. A Report by the American Psychological Association Zero Tolerance Task Force. www.apa.org/pubs/reports/zero tolerance-report.pdf

Slavin, R. E. (1999). How can funding equity ensure enhanced achievement? *Journal of Education Finance, 24*, 520. www.jstor.org/stable/40704081

Stringer, C. (2012). *Lone survivors: How we came to be the only humans on earth*. St. Martin's Press

Sutcher, L., Darling-Hammond, L., & Carver-Thomas, D. (2016). *A coming crisis in teaching? Teacher supply, demand, and shortages in the U.S.* Learning Policy Institute. https://doi.org/10.54300/247.242

Toro, J. D., & Wang, M. (2021). *The role of suspensions of minor infractions and school climate in predicting academic performance among adolescents.* American Psychological Association.

U.S. Office of Management and Budget. (1978). Office of Management and Budget. *Directive No. 15: Race and ethnic standards for Federal statistics and administrative reporting.* Centers for Disease Control and Prevention. https://wonder.cdc.gov/wonder/help/populations/bridged-race/Directive15.html

4

UNMET NEEDS OF YOUTH WITH MENTAL, EMOTIONAL, AND BEHAVIORAL HEALTH DISORDERS

Like adverse nationwide school-level practices, the unmet needs of youth with mental, emotional, and behavioral health disorders (MEB) can play a pivotal role in their entrance into the school-to-prison pipeline (STPP). Estimates indicate that only 24% of children with mental health needs actually receive treatment, and the gap is even greater for African Americans than for White Americans. In this country, people typically wait until MEB disorders emerge, attempt to treat them, and then either cure them or try to limit the damage they cause. These efforts usually involve any number of expensive interventions, ranging from psychiatric care to incarceration (National Research Council and Institute of Medicine, 2009). This chapter examines the needs of children with MEB disorders and the potential effect these disorders have on a child's entrance into the STPP.

Mental Health in the United States

In 1999, the Office of the U.S. Surgeon General published its first comprehensive report on mental health in the United States (U.S. Department of Health and Human Services). This report increased public awareness of the importance of mental health and well-being, and of their relationship to improving the overall health of the nation. It also used a scientific and empirical approach to address the full spectrum of mental health

DOI: 10.4324/9781003284383-6

issues, including mental health promotion, prevention of mental illness, and treatment of mental health problems across an individual's lifespan. This document discusses five overarching themes:

1. Mental health promotion and mental illness prevention require a public health approach. Such an approach requires not only diagnosis and treatment of illness but also epidemiological studies of the population to prevent disorders. This approach also promotes health and well-being, increases access to services, and evaluates those services.

2. Mental disorders are disabling, and the burdens they impose on individuals and entire countries have been greatly underestimated.

3. The concepts of mental health and mental illness are to be viewed on a continuum of functioning. Mental health refers to an individual's ability to successfully perform tasks of living, such as being productive, forming healthy relationships, and being able to cope with change and adversity. Mental illness refers to all diagnosable mental disorders that are identified by changes in mood, thought, and behavior that create impaired functioning.

4. The mind and body are integral to each other and to physical and mental well-being. The integration of mental and physical health is critically important to one's overall health and the health of the nation.

5. Stigma exerts a major influence on several dimensions of mental health care. Stigma and a lack of understanding of mental health disorders can prevent people from seeking psychological help and can lead to reduced funding for mental health treatment and prevention services. Additionally, stigma and misconceptions can result in the ostracism of individuals with mental health disorders from their families and communities.

Several aspects of these overarching themes are addressed in this chapter, particularly those that focus on epidemiological studies, the burdens MEB disorders impose on individuals, and the impact stigma and insufficient knowledge about mental health disorders have on preventing people from seeking psychological help.

In 2001, The Office of the Surgeon General (US) further detailed the theme of stigma and misconceptions in the supplemental report *Mental Health: Culture, Race, and Ethnicity*, focusing on mental health and culture, race, and ethnicity. Among the major themes were the role of these factors in the promotion of mental health and the treatment of mental illness, and the disparities in mental health care and services among populations of color within the United States. To address the stigma specifically associated with the term "mental disorder," the Committee on the Prevention of Mental Disorders and Substance Abuse Among Children, Youth, and Young Adults adopted the term "mental, emotional, and behavioral disorders" (MEB) in 2009 to encompass the disorders diagnosed according to the Diagnostic and Statistical Manual of Mental Disorders, 4th Edition (DSM-IV) criteria (National Research Council and Institute of Medicine, 2009). The use of the term mental, emotional, and behavioral disorders, however, has not been universally adopted in the scientific literature, and the term mental disorder continues to be used. Since this is the case, both terms are used in this book interchangeably.

As is indicated earlier, mental health and mental illness are to be viewed on a continuum of functioning. Mental health refers to an individual's ability to successfully perform tasks of living, such as being productive, forming healthy relationships, and coping with change and adversity. Mental illness refers to all diagnosable MEB disorders that are identified by changes in mood, thought, and behavior that create impaired functioning (National Research Council and Institute of Medicine, 2009). The Diagnostic and Statistical Manual of Mental Disorders, 5th Edition (DSM-5), defines MEB disorders as a syndrome characterized by clinically significant disturbance in an individual's cognition, emotion regulation, or behavior that reflects a dysfunction in the psychological, biological, or developmental processes underlying mental functioning. They are usually associated with significant distress or disability in social, occupational, or other important activities. These diagnosable MEB disorders are made by psychiatrists and other physicians, psychologists, social workers, nurses, counselors, forensic and legal specialists, occupational and rehabilitation therapists, and other health professionals (2013).

In addition to increasing public awareness of the importance of mental health and well-being, the Office of the U.S. Surgeon General (2001) also spearheaded a wealth of research studies about the mental health of school-aged children. Research now shows that most MEB health disorders have their roots in childhood and youth. Children and adolescents with MEB health disorders exhibit a wide range of behavioral and social characteristics, including externalizing and internalizing behavior patterns. Externalizing behavior problems are typically characterized by verbal and physical aggression, coercive tactics, and delinquent acts. Internalizing behavior problems are manifested by conditions such as depression, anxiety, social isolation, somatic complaints, and obsessive–compulsive disorder. Among adults reporting an MEB health disorder during their lifetime, more than half reported the onset as occurring in childhood or adolescence. As a result, the potential lifetime benefits of preventing MEB health disorders are greatest by focusing on young people, since early interventions can be effective in delaying or preventing the onset of such disorders (National Research Council and Institute of Medicine, 2009).

Prevalence of Mental, Emotional, and Behavioral Health Disorders in Youth

According to the National Research Council and Institute of Medicine, 14% to 20% of children and adolescents living in the United States (up to 1 out of 5) experience an MEB health disorder for which an estimated $247 billion is spent each year (2009). In fact, mental illness is the most prevalent chronic health condition experienced by youth (Melchert, 2015). According to Merikangas et al. (2010), one out of eight children ages 8 to 15 (13.1%) met the criteria for an MEB in 2010, and 11.3% met the criteria for an MEB disorder with severe impairment.

In a 2013 report published by the Center for Disease Control and Prevention (CDC), it was revealed that attention-deficit/hyperactivity disorder (6.8%) was the most prevalent parent-reported diagnosis among children aged 3–17 years, followed by behavioral or conduct problems (3.5%), anxiety (3.0%), depression (2.1%), autism spectrum disorders (1.1%), and Tourette syndrome (0.2% among children aged 6–17 years).

Mental, emotional, and behavioral health disorders such as depression, conduct disorders, and substance abuse among children, youth, and young adults create an enormous burden for the youth themselves, their families, and the nation. These disorders are also important public health issues in the United States because of their prevalence and early onset. The results of a survey of adults revealed that half of all lifetime cases of diagnosable mental illness began by age 14 and three fourths by age 24 (Kessler et al., 2005). According to Hadorn (1991), however, the basic tendency in America is to focus on the rule of rescue, which he described as a powerful human proclivity to rescue endangered life. As a society, he said, we suffer from a collective health care myopia, and we have not yet figured out how to balance rescue, which is after-the-fact treatment and much more costly, with the less dramatic but often far less costly prevention of the onset of the problem.

In the book *Preventing Mental, Emotional, and Behavioral Disorders Among Young People* (2009), the concerns addressed in this chapter were summarized in this manner:

> MEB disorders in young people are a public health concern because they cause suffering to individuals and their families, limit the ability to reach normal goals for social and educational achievement, increase the risk of further psychopathology, functional impairment, and suboptimal functioning throughout life, and impose heavy costs on society because of the resultant need for extra care, the social disruption that they can cause, and the risk that affected young people will underperform as adults. The significant economic costs of treating disorders warrant an increased focus on preventing them. However, support for prevention programs depends on knowing the size of the problem and its societal burden and on being able to monitor reductions in that burden when prevention programs are put into place. The United States is significantly behind other countries in supporting the necessary information-gathering programs.
>
> (p. 36)

Mental health costs are often hidden from national accounting methods because a major portion of these costs do not take place in mental health care settings, accruing instead to such systems as education, juvenile justice, and physical health care. The early onset of MEB disorders frequently results in lower school achievement, an increased burden on the child welfare system, and greater demands on the juvenile justice system. In fact, it is estimated that more than one quarter of the total costs for mental health treatment services among adolescents are incurred in the education and juvenile justice systems, with the total annual economic costs in 2007 at roughly $247 billion. Youth with emotional and behavioral problems are also at a greatly increased risk of psychiatric and substance abuse problems. In terms of alcohol abuse alone, it was found that the earlier young people start drinking, the more likely they are to have serious alcohol dependence as adults (National Research Council and Institute of Medicine, 2009).

Trauma

The DSM-5 offers a common language and standard criteria for the classification of MEB disorders. It is used by mental health clinicians, researchers, health insurance companies, the legal system, and policy makers. Since its first publication in 1952, the DSM has incrementally added to the total number of MEB disorders and removed any that no longer qualify. In the 1980s, the American Psychiatric Association added the term post-traumatic stress disorder (PTSD) to this manual, primarily in response to mental health problems among Vietnam War veterans. Prior to this, the symptoms had gone by different names, such as "soldier's heart," "shell shock," "battle fatigue," and "combat stress" (Schmid, 2017).

In the DSM-5, post-traumatic stress disorder warrants a close examination because it is unlike most of the MEB disorders seen in youth where the etiology or cause is frequently unknown. PTSD typically results from exposure to traumatic events, such as witnessing or experiencing physical or sexual abuse, violence in families and communities, the loss of a loved one, refugee and war situations, life with a family member whose caregiving ability is impaired, or a life-threatening injury or illness. As is indicated in Chapter 1, trauma is another factor to consider in a child's susceptibility to the STPP. Most children and adolescents in the

United States do not suffer from or experience violent traumas or mental health problems. However, reviews of detained and incarcerated youthful offenders have found significantly higher incidences of these experiences among young people who end up in the nation's detention and incarceration facilities (Mallett, 2016). The first large-scale longitudinal study of the mental health needs and outcomes of juvenile detainees conducted by Teplin et al. (2013) found that of the 1,829 randomly selected youth who participated in this study, 93% experienced one or more traumas in their lifetime, and more than 1 in 10 detainees met diagnostic criteria for post-traumatic stress disorder during the year prior to their interview. Of this group, 46% of the males and 57% of the females had two or more psychiatric disorders.

According to the National Child Traumatic Stress Network, children who suffer from traumatic stress are those who are exposed to one or more traumas over the course of their lives and develop reactions that persist and affect their daily lives after the traumatic events have ended (2003). It is estimated that 26% of children in the United States will witness or experience a traumatic event before the age of 4 years (Briggs-Gowan et al., 2010), but because of various factors, such as resilience or a caring and supportive environment, not all of these children will develop PTSD. In terms of comorbidity, however, clinical and epidemiologic studies have established that PTSD is highly comorbid with other mental disorders (Koenen et al., 2008). For instance, many children who are diagnosed as having PTSD or acute stress disorder also meet criteria for attention-deficit/hyperactivity disorder and mood disorders, such as depression and oppositional defiant disorder (National Child Traumatic Stress Network, 2003). This is very important diagnostically and also in terms of treatment efficacy. For example, if a child or adolescent has been diagnosed and treated for PTSD but should have been diagnosed and treated for an oppositional defiant disorder as well, it is doubtful that even the most well-researched, evidence-based, mental health treatment protocol will keep him or her from entering the STPP.

Unmet Needs of Youth with MEB Disorders

National surveys show that most youth who could potentially benefit from mental health services do not receive them, even though evidence-based treatment options are available. Estimates indicate that only 24% of children with mental health needs actually receive treatment, and the gap is even greater for African Americans than for White Americans. Of those children who do receive care, three fourths receive it within the school system (National Research Council and Institute of Medicine, 2009), which (as this book indicates) may not fully address the complexity of their needs. As is indicated previously, research indicates that children commonly have more than one MEB. For example, Armstrong and Costello (2002) found that the odds of children having an attention-deficit/hyperactivity disorder are 10 times more likely if a child has a conduct or oppositional defiant disorder. The odds of having a substance use disorder are eight times more likely if a child has a conduct or oppositional defiant disorder, and the odds of having an anxiety disorder are eight times more likely if a child has depression. In addition, it was found that there is significant comorbidity among disruptive behavior disorders, attention-deficit/hyperactivity disorder, substance abuse disorders, and emotional disorders (anxiety and depression). Comorbidity studies examining behavior problems revealed that early aggressive behavior greatly increases the risk of conduct disorders, drug use, and other externalizing behaviors, while environmental and individual-level protective factors and preventive interventions can reduce these risks. Therefore, when left unmet, MEB disorders are linked to costly negative outcomes such as academic and behavioral problems, dropping out of school (National Research Council and Institute of Medicine, 2009), the STPP, and delinquency.

Striking Disparities and Greater Disability Burden on African Americans

According to the U.S. Department of Education, African American children are almost three times more likely than White children to be labeled as having a mental disorder and almost twice as likely to be labeled as having an emotional/behavioral disorder (Losen & Orfield, 2002). Ironically, striking disparities in mental health care are also found for racial minorities when compared with Whites. In general, minorities have less access to and availability of mental health services and are less likely to receive them when needed. Additionally, minorities in treatment often receive a poorer quality of mental health care and are underrepresented in mental health research. These disparities impose a greater disability burden on minorities from mental illness than they do Whites.

The report *Mental Health: Culture, Race, and Ethnicity* (2001) summarized these disparities when it described how, by not receiving effective treatment, minorities have greater levels of disability in terms of lost workdays and limitations in daily activities. Minorities are also overrepresented among the nation's most vulnerable populations and have higher rates of mental disorders and more barriers to care. Collectively, these disparate lines of evidence support the finding that minorities suffer a disproportionately high disability burden from unmet mental health needs. The greater disability burden has real consequences, such as the inability to completely share in the hope afforded by remarkable scientific advances in the understanding and treatment of MEB disorders. Most troubling of all, however, is that the burden on minorities is growing. Minorities in the United States are becoming more populous, all the while experiencing continuing inequality in income and economic opportunity. They face a social and economic environment of inequality that includes greater exposure to racism and discrimination, violence, and poverty, all of which take a toll on mental health. In addition, a constellation of barriers deters minorities from reaching treatment, such as cost, fragmentation of services, lack of availability of services, and societal stigma toward mental illness. Additional barriers include mistrust and fear of treatment, racism and discrimination, and differences in language and communication.

This report made a poignant point about communication, which for centuries African Americans were forbidden from doing during slavery, when it asserted that the ability for consumers and providers to communicate with one another is essential for all aspects of health care. Yet, this report indicated, it carries special significance in the area of mental health because mental disorders affect thoughts, moods, and the highest integrative aspects of behavior. The diagnosis and treatment of mental, emotional, and behavioral disorders greatly depend on verbal communication and trust between patient and clinician. More broadly, mental health care disparities may also stem from minorities' historical and current struggles with racism and discrimination, which affect their mental health and contribute to their lower economic, social, and political status.

"The cumulative weight and interplay of all barriers to care, not any single one alone, is likely responsible for mental health disparities" (Department of Health and Human Services, 1999, p. 4).

Very Young Children

In addition to the previously mentioned barriers that deter minorities from receiving treatment, Giordano et al. (2017) reported that a prominent obstacle in addressing childhood mental health needs is that many people have erroneous ideas about mental health in children. One common myth, for example, is that children do not experience mental health problems. In reality, however, young children can and do experience symptoms of poor mental health, even to the point of clinical diagnosis. In their article, they wrote that diagnosis in young children is complicated by the fact that, for many mental health problems, early childhood symptoms manifest differently from those seen in adults, or even those seen in older children or adolescents. As a result of this, symptoms can be overlooked, even by mental health providers.

A second myth is that mental health problems in young children, particularly externalizing difficulties, are just manifestations of bad parenting that need to be corrected. While parenting practices and family variables play a role in the development of mental, emotional, and behavioral health problems in children, such problems result from a confluence of factors, including biological and environmental influences, that cannot just be dismissed as bad parenting. Third, there is the myth that early childhood mental, emotional, and behavioral health problems represent a developmental phase that children will simply grow out of. While some young children do experience delays or difficulties that are short-term and confined to a particular developmental period, there are many who show trajectories of persistent or worsening problems over time. Another prominent obstacle to addressing mental health problems during early childhood is the lack of cohesive public policy. Mental health policies and funding are more likely to target older children, adolescents, and adults.

Public health approaches, which encompass prevention, hold promise as mechanisms for expanding services to younger children, but they require more widespread implementation and sustained support. In addition, Giordano et al. (2017) indicated that gaps in public policy are related to other obstacles in promoting early childhood mental health, such as the lack of a solid national initiative calling for services to younger children. This means that families seeking such services often encounter a fragmented system in which effective interventions might not be available or are not covered by insurance. Establishing a coordinated network of early childhood mental health services also lacks the personnel who have sufficient knowledge and training to provide such services. However, although these obstacles in addressing the mental health needs of very young children are indeed substantial, they are not insurmountable, especially when one considers the importance of early intervention and what is at stake for children and adolescents who do not receive the support they need and enter the STPP instead.

References

American Psychiatric Association. (2013). *DSM-5 task force*, 5th ed. American Psychiatric Publishing, Inc. https://doi.org/10.1176/appi.books.9780890425596

Armstrong, T. D., & Costello, E. J. (2002). Community studies on adolescent substance use, abuse, or dependence and psychiatric comorbidity. *Journal of Consulting and Clinical Psychology, 70*(6), 1224–1239. https://pubmed.ncbi.nlm.nih.gov/12472299/

Briggs-Gowan, M. J., Ford, J. D., Fraleigh, L., McCarthy, K., & Carter, A. S. (2010, December 23). Prevalence of exposure to potentially traumatic events in a healthy birth cohort of very young children in the northeastern United States. *Journal of Traumatic Stress, 23*(6), 725–733. https://doi.org/10.1002/jts.20593.

Giordano, K., Garro, A., Rosen, G., & Gubi, A. (2017). Early childhood mental health and the school psychologist. *Communique, 46*(3), 1, 27–30.

Hadorn, D. C. (1991). Setting health care priorities in Oregon: Cost-effectiveness meets the rule of rescue. *The Journal of the American Medical Association, 265*(17), 2218–2225.

Kessler, R. C., Berglund, P., Demler, O., Jin, R., Merikangas, K. R., & Walters, E. E. (2005). Lifetime prevalence and age-of-onset distributions of DSM-IV disorders in the national comorbidity survey replication. *Archives of General Psychiatry, 62*(6), 593–602.

Koenen, K. C., Moffitt, T. E., Caspi, A., Harriton, G., & Poulton, R. (2008, May). The developmental mental-disorder histories of adults with posttraumatic stress disorder: A prospective longitudinal birth cohort study. *Journal of Abnormal Psychology, 117*(2), 460–466. https://doi.org/10.1037/0021-843x.

Losen, D. J., & Orfield, G. (2002). *Racial inequity in special education*. Harvard Education Publishing Group.

Mallett, C. A. (2016). *The school-to-prison pipeline, A comprehensive assessment*. Springer Publishing Company.

Melchert, T. P. (2015). *Biopsychosocial practice: A science-based framework for behavioral health care*. American Psychological Association.

Merikangas, K. R., He, J. P., Burstein, M., Swanson, S. A., Avenevoli, S., Cui, L., Benjet, C., Georgiades, K., & Swendsen, J. (2010, October). Lifetime prevalence of mental disorders in U.S. adolescents: Results from the National Comorbidity Survey

Replication-Adolescent Supplement. *Journal of the American Academy of Child & Adolescent Psychiatry, 49*(10). https://doi.org/10.1016/j.jaac.2010.05.017.

National Child Traumatic Stress Network. (2003). *What is child traumatic stress?* www.nctsn.org/sites/default/files/resources//what_is_child_traumatic_stress.pdf

National Research Council and Institute of Medicine. (2009). *Preventing mental, emotional, and behavioral disorders among young people: Progress and possibilities.* The National Academies Press. https://doi.org/10.17226/12480

Office of the Surgeon General (US); Center for Mental Health Services (US); National Institute of Mental Health (US). (2001, August). *Mental health: Culture, race, and ethnicity: A supplement to mental health: A report of the surgeon general.* Substance Abuse and Mental Health Services Administration (US). www.ncbi.nlm.nih.gov/books/NBK44243/

Schmid, J. (2017, March 17). From generation to generation: An epidemic of childhood trauma haunts Milwaukee. *The Milwaukee Journal Sentinel.* https://projects.jsonline.com/news/2017/3/23/epidemic-of-childhood-trauma-haunts-milwaukee.html

Teplin, L. A., Abram, K. M., Washburn, Welty, L. J., Hershfield, J. A., & Dulcan, M. K. (2013). *The Northwestern juvenile project: Overview.* Office of Juvenile Justice and Delinquency Prevention

U. S. Department of Health and Human Services. (1999). *Mental health: A report of the surgeon General.* U. S. Department of Health and Human Services, Substance Abuse and Mental Health Service Administration, Center for Mental Health Services.

5

EXPLICIT AND IMPLICIT BIAS—THREATS TO THE FABRIC OF ETHICAL PRACTICE

The previous chapters examined the history of the school-to-prison pipeline (STPP) and how unmet mental, emotional, and behavioral health disorders in youth and questionable court and school-based practices increase the chances of a child entering this pipeline. But, as is indicated in Chapter 1, entrance into the STPP can also result from disparities in the application of discipline based on race, which is an ethical issue. These disparities can be linked to the explicit and implicit biases (which all people have) of teachers, administrators, mental health providers, and others who work with children. This chapter examines these biases, how they develop and are sustained, and the threat they pose to ethical practice.

Education is one of the most honorable professions in the world, but in the school system, subjective or individual biases pose significant ethical threats to the objectivity and fairness of trained professionals, such as teachers, mental health providers, and administrators. This chapter describes what explicit and implicit biases are, explains why they pose such significant challenges to objectivity and fairness, and examines how they threaten the "fabric" of ethical practice for all professionals in the school setting. All humans have explicit and implicit biases, but in the public school system, negative biases toward African American children can have adverse, long-term consequences and funnel these children into the STPP.

DOI: 10.4324/9781003284383-7

Prejudice, Discrimination, and Explicit and Implicit Bias

Prejudice is an unfavorable attitude toward a group of people and is usually associated with discrimination. Discrimination is unequal treatment of different groups, such as minority groups, the physically disabled, or people who are obese, lesbian, gay, bisexual, or transgender (Kalat, 2017). Although prejudice and discrimination toward African Americans have been ubiquitous problems in the United States for several centuries, the scientific study of prejudice did not occur until the publication of *The Nature of Prejudice* by Allport in 1954. Allport was one of the first psychologists to study personality and is often referred to as one of the founding figures of personality psychology. Many of the current scientific studies about prejudice and discrimination are outgrowths of Allport's work and, in part, the result of recent changes in human values and social justice initiatives of many Americans. According to Banaji and Greenwald (2013), these changes in values and aspirations occurred within the last few generations and have their origins in what they call "our conscious, reflective minds." Our conscious and reflective minds, they contend, have transformed our sense of what is fair, just, and the right way to live as social beings.

Counterintuitively, the civil rights movement of the 1950s and 1960s was also a contributing factor to the changes in human values and aspirations, and the United States' position in the world as a model country for equality, freedom, and justice played a significant part. The civil rights movement revealed the struggles of African Americans to achieve basic human rights that were equal to those of White Americans. Equality in those things that most Whites took for granted, such as opportunities in employment, housing, and education, as well as the right to vote, the right of equal access to public facilities, and the right to be free of racial discrimination and terrorization, were passionately addressed during the civil rights movement. Violence, which was fueled by racist beliefs, was a frequent response to nonviolent civil rights protests. This violence was televised internationally by the media, which highlighted major flaws in how democracy was practiced in America for African Americans. The ideals of democracy that were and continue to be promoted internationally make democracy the best form of government in the world. But it was quickly realized during the civil rights movement that it was difficult if not impossible to promote these ideals internationally if they were not practiced at home.

Decades have passed since the end of the civil rights movement, and human values and aspirations have certainly changed, but prejudice and racial discrimination continue to be chronic and pervasive parts of the life experiences of people of color (Alvarez et al., 2016; Sue et al., 2019; Kendi, 2019). Prejudice and discriminatory behavior result from bias, which may be explicit or implicit. Explicit bias reflects the attitudes or beliefs that one endorses at a conscious level, so the individual is aware of his or her feelings and sometimes the motivations behind his or her behaviors.

Several decades ago, many Americans admitted their prejudices and discriminatory opinions and beliefs openly through racial slurs and bigoted statements (Kalat, 2017). These individuals are typically referred to as racists. They are characterized by prejudicial beliefs in the superiority and entitlement of their race over others (although, as is indicated in Chapter 1, there is only one race, which is the human race), bigotry, and by discriminatory actions and violence toward people they believe are of other races or ethnicities. The vehemence of these prejudicial beliefs, discriminatory actions, and violence were captured countless times by the media during the civil rights movement in the 1950s and 1960s and, regrettably, were not new or isolated events in the United States. In the book *Race, Religion, and the Continuing American Dilemma*, Lincoln (1984) asserted that the most obvious feature of contemporary American life is violence, which began with the effort to exterminate the Indian, and the protracted effort to dehumanize the African American. Violence has been confirmed as a way of life, he said, and neither human life nor human dignity is characteristically sacred because it has always been bought and sold with impunity, whether at the slave-auction block, or in the courtrooms, or through a thousand sophisticated strategies designed to exploit whatever values the White man recognized in the black condition.

The vehemence of prejudicial beliefs, discriminatory actions, and violence have spawned the collection of hate crime data by the United States.

The U.S. Department of Justice Federal Bureau of Investigation's (FBI) Uniform Crime Reporting (UCR) program recently released 2020's Hate Crime Statistics. The UCR program serves as the national repository for crime data voluntarily collected and submitted by law enforcement (U.S. Department of Justice, 2022). In total, 15,138 law enforcement agencies submitted reports documenting 8,263 hate crimes. Most, or 61.8%, of these single-bias incidents were hate crimes that were based on race, ethnicity, or ancestry bias. African Americans made up more than half of the victims. The number of reported hate crimes against African Americans rose from 1,972 in 2019 to 2,871 in 2020 (Burch & Ploeg, 2022).

Americans share a collective belief that racial and ethnic discrimination is morally wrong. However, they divide along racial lines on the question of whether racial and ethnic discrimination continue to occur today and whether one's race or ethnicity matters (Matthew, 2015). Americans who are members of minority groups, such as African and Asian Americans, all report to varying degrees that race still matters and that racial discrimination is alive and well. Few Whites, on the other hand, believe that race is an important consideration in American life. In addition, over 95% of White Americans who were asked believe they are racially unbiased (Pew Research Center, 2013). These data help explain why it is so difficult to objectively discuss issues related to race in the United States and effect meaningful change in many policies and practices that adversely affect African Americans.

In her book *Race and Racism*, Golash-Boza (2019) makes a distinction between old racism (which permitted the internment of Japanese Americans and the enslavement of Africans) and a new but related ideology which she calls *new racism*. In new racism, she contends, it is no longer acceptable to make overtly racist statements or to have overtly racist laws and practices that are explicitly racist. Similar to the book *The New Jim Crow* (Alexander, 2012), Golash-Boza (2019) believes that new racism is an outgrowth of past racial inequality, mass media, and popular beliefs, which makes the new racism appear natural, normal, and inevitable. As a result, racial inequality in the United States has become naturalized because we have normalized the overrepresentation of African American men among prisoners and White men among the elite, even though we would never accept laws that overtly discriminated against African Americans.

Unlike explicit bias, unconscious or implicit bias is bias in judgment and/or behavior that results from subtle cognitive processes, such as implicit attitudes and implicit stereotypes. Implicit bias often operates at a level below conscious awareness and without intentional control. These attitudes or stereotypes affect our understanding, actions, and decisions. They are activated involuntarily, without awareness or intentional control, and can be either positive or negative. Research from the neuro, social, and cognitive sciences shows that hidden biases are distressingly pervasive and influence the ways in which we see and treat others, even when we are determined to be fair and objective (Staats et al., 2016). Thus, people act much more in accordance with their implicit or subconsciously held attitudes and beliefs, and much less in accordance with what they say they believe or intend (Matthew, 2015).

Implicit biases form and inform our perceptions, judgments, and conduct toward people from identifiable ethnic and racial groups. According to the book *Just Medicine: A Cure for Racial Inequality in American Health Care* (Matthew, 2015), the first step in the development of implicit biases involves storing social knowledge, which occurs throughout the lifetime. The second step occurs the moment two people meet. Americans live in a race-conscious society and instinctively identify the group to which another person belongs and give a positive or negative value to that individual or group based on stereotypes. These stereotypes inform the overt judgments that ultimately direct how we perceive, judge, and relate to people of different racial and ethnic groups. The underlying attitudes and stereotypes that lead to implicit bias or beliefs are simple associations that a person makes between an object or individual and the subsequent evaluation of that object or individual that is automatically activated by its mere presence (National Association of School Psychologists, 2017).

In the book *The First R: How Children Learn Race and Racism*, it was revealed that the vulnerability associated with implicit bias develops at an early age, is reinforced by the beliefs and assumptions of our respective communities, and is perpetuated by stereotypes presented in the mass media (Van Ausdale & Feagin, 2001). These stereotypes, Carter et al.

(2014) contend, are developed through centuries of oppression and discrimination, and are "rooted" in our national consciousness.

Why Does Implicit Bias Matter?

According to Staats et al. (2016), implicit biases matter because they can affect decisions, behaviors, and interactions with others. While most research focuses on implicit bias through the lens of White individuals, as is indicated earlier, everyone is vulnerable to it. However, historically, it has been African Americans who are portrayed in movies and television in unfavorable and demeaning roles, such as those associated with crime, drugs, and other types of negativities. As these images and stereotypes are repeatedly reinforced by other movies and television programs, an inherent fear of African American individuals subconsciously develops, which makes African Americans particularly vulnerable to the effects of implicit bias (National Association of School Psychologists, 2017).

Implicit bias presents a unique challenge for individuals who work with school-aged children because it operates on an unconscious level and is neither deliberate nor intentional. As is indicated previously, it manifests as an automatic, stereotypical response or association made about an individual or group of individuals based on perceived group membership. Often, these associations are related to race. As is indicated in Chapter 1, race is easily identifiable when the child or adolescent is African American, which makes these individuals easy targets if the observer is susceptible to negatively biased perceptions of African Americans. For example, a study conducted by Goff et al. (2014) found that African American boys are especially vulnerable to implicit biases because they are typically perceived as being older and more dangerous than their White counterparts. *Girlhood Interrupted: The Erasure of Black Girls' Childhood* (Epstein et al., 2017), a similar study, looked at African American females. This groundbreaking study provided, for the first time, data showing that adults also view African American girls as less innocent and more adult-like than their White peers, especially in the age range of 5–14. These factors can negatively influence the observer's perception of these children, even when altruistic intentions are present.

Implicit Bias and Educators/Teachers

Although there is considerable variation in the responsibilities placed on educators throughout this country, federal, state, and local governments still rely on their impartiality, objectivity, and egalitarian intentions to educate each child. As is stated earlier in this chapter, education is one of the most noble professions in the world, but it is also a complex and dynamic system that provides many opportunities for implicit biases to emerge (Staats et al., 2016). School punishments, for instance, are not always equitably distributed, even though zero tolerance disciplinary policies have attempted to standardize the consequences for unruly children and adolescents in most public schools across the nation. This disparity is, in part, due to educators' implicit bias. Teachers play a pivotal role in who is referred to the principal's office for disciplinary infractions, and these referrals sometimes result in school suspension, expulsion, and a variety of other negative outcomes. For example, low-income students are much more likely to be punished in school than others (McNulty-Eitle & Eitle, 2004; Skiba et al., 2000). Since implicit biases often go unexamined and are hidden, especially when an individual is faced with ambiguous and subjective situations (Girvan et al., 2017; Staats, 2016), these biases can operate without the observer's awareness but remain as sinister as bacteria in a petri dish during a laboratory study at a medical facility.

As is indicated in Chapter 1, hundreds of thousands of middle and high school students are caught every year within the school-to-prison pipeline through suspensions, arrests by school resource officers, and expulsions (U. S. Department of Education, 2022). A single suspension or expulsion from school doubles the risk of a student repeating a grade, which is also a strong risk factor for the student dropping out of high school (Kang-Brown et al., 2013; Rich-Shae & Fox, 2014) and entering the STPP. Research reveals that African American students, especially boys, are disciplined more often and receive more out-of-school suspensions and expulsions than White students. This is not a new phenomenon. For more than three decades, African American male students have been affected by exclusionary school disciplinary practices, such as office referrals, suspensions, school-based arrests, alternative learning environments, and expulsions (Achilles et al., 2007; Skiba et al., 2002). Contrary to a prevailing assumption that African American boys are just getting what they deserve, research shows that these boys do not act out in the classroom any more than their White peers. There are, however, differences in the behaviors these two groups display. White students are significantly more likely than African American students to be referred to the office for smoking, leaving without permission, vandalism, and obscene language. African American students, on the other hand, are more likely to be referred for disrespect, excessive noise, threats, and loitering. No support was found for the hypothesis that African American students act out more than other students. Rather, African American students appear to be referred to the office for less serious and more subjective reasons. Coupled with extensive and highly consistent prior data, these results argue that the disproportionate representation of African Americans in office referrals, suspension, and expulsion is evidence of a pervasive and systematic bias that may well be inherent in the use of exclusionary discipline (Skiba et al., 2000).

In a blistering assessment of the United States' involvement in racial discipline disparities, Carter et al. (2014) indicated that the disparities are a consequence of both current and historical factors that have shaped school life in this country. They contend that the ravages of slavery and Jim Crow forced migration and policies that enforced unequal treatment of African Americans at an economic and social disadvantage that persists to this day. History, they stated, left us with the current pervasive and false ideas about "races" that have shaped our perceptions of who is valued and who is not, who is capable and who is not, and who is "safe" and who is "dangerous." Because many Americans have such difficulty talking about issues of race and ethnicity in a frank and open manner, we are left with ideas about race that still prompt exclusionary and disparate disciplinary practices, and segregated, boundaried experiences that make it challenging to confront racial issues, even as those issues continue to play out in our everyday interactions.

Implicit Bias and Mental Health Providers

The term implicit bias was first coined by social psychologists Banaji and Greenwald in 1995 (Cherry, 2019), but little research has been conducted about implicit bias as it relates to psychologists and other mental health providers. This is an unfortunate oversight because mental health providers are frequently the first point of contact troubled children with mental, emotional, and behavioral (MEB) health problems have with the mental health community. Typically, this contact happens within the public school system, which is the most common entry point to mental health services for youth (Brock, 2015).

As is indicated earlier in this chapter, implicit bias presents a unique challenge for individuals who work with school-aged children because it operates on an unconscious level and is neither deliberate nor intentional. In 2003, Snowden, a graduate school professor at the University of California, Berkeley School of Public Health, wrote there may be greater reason for concern regarding bias in mental health as compared to other areas of health. Although consensus has increased about appropriate methods of diagnosis and treatment, a large role remains for discretion. In addition, there is great variation in practice norms, and the advent of well-founded protocols is recent. These protocols, however, are far from achieving full acceptance by all mental health professionals.

Protocols in psychological practice are important, but they too can be compromised by implicit biases. The first scientific study revealing this was conducted by Bartholomew (1987), a graduate psychology student at the University of Southern Mississippi. The Wechsler Intelligence Scale for Children-Revised (WISC-R; Wechsler, 1974), a structured intelligence measure with specific protocols the examiner must follow during its administration, interpretation, and scoring, was used to determine whether scoring bias exists. In this study, four male children (two African Americans and two Whites) were screened for dialectal variations by seven doctoral-level speech communication or speech pathology experts. Audiotapes were produced by these four children, who used identical responses (except for dialectical variations) to ambiguous responses on the Similarities, Vocabulary, and Comprehension subtests. The dialectal variations included Black Nonstandard, Black Standard, White Nonstandard, and White Standard speech, which were evaluated as such by two doctoral-level communication specialists.

Identical audiotaped responses were produced by the respondents, which were then scored by 59 subjects using WISC-R scoring criteria. The subjects were graduate psychology students or practicing psychologists with an average of 5.5 years of work experience. The subjects were placed into one of four experimental conditions, with each condition combining a message attribute (standard or nonstandard) and speaker attribute (Black or White). The four conditions were Nonstandard/Black, Standard/Black, Nonstandard/White, and Standard/White. Results revealed that examiners (subjects) did not differentially score children who used an African American dialect or children who used nonstandard English. Statistical significance was, however, obtained on the Similarities subtest with the White examiners (subjects) giving a significantly higher average score to the White examinees than they gave to the African American examinees and African American (subjects) giving significantly lower scores to the White examinees (Bartholomew, 1987). Thus, this study confirmed that implicit bias in mental health is a grave concern in the provision of direct services to patients or clients, even when rigid protocols are in place.

One of the most recent examinations of implicit bias along the mental health care continuum was published online on March 1, 2018, as an open forum by Merino et al. According to this forum, research showed that implicit bias is prevalent among service providers and is automatically activated during practitioner-client encounters. The authors indicated that despite conscious efforts to provide equitable care to all patients, at least two-thirds of health providers hold some form of implicit bias against marginalized groups. This bias can negatively influence a provider's willingness to engage in patient-centered care, provide referrals to specialized treatment, or even adhere to evidence-based guidelines. Mental health systems are particularly vulnerable to the negative effects of implicit bias because the diagnosis and treatment of mental health conditions rely heavily on provider discretion. As suggested by Snowden (2003), providers' unconscious attitudes about groups, such as homeless persons, veterans, people of color, or incarcerated individuals, among others, can have multiple negative consequences for individuals seeking mental health treatment.

> Implicit bias can preclude certain groups from accessing mental health services. Unlike other types of health care that use an interprofessional, team-based approach, mental health services

are frequently provided on a one-on-one basis, so that a single provider is the gatekeeper to accessing care. Thus, there is perhaps a greater potential for implicit bias among mental health professionals that prevents certain groups from accessing some mental health services.

(Merino, Adams, & Hall, para. 3)

Being aware of the potential impact implicit bias can have on one's perceptions, decisions, and behaviors is a healthy perspective of the general public in the United States. This country's heinous history toward African Americans and the continuation of hate crimes make a response such as indifference troubling, since it can easily be mistaken for complicity by perpetrators. But this awareness goes much further for professional educators and mental health providers who work with children and adolescents. Explicit and implicit bias are particularly dangerous in these situations because they can prevent some of the most vulnerable children from accessing the mental health support that they need, threaten the fabric of ethical practice, which demands objectivity and is the hallmark of every scientific effort, and increase a troubled child's chances of entering the STPP.

References

Achilles, G. M., McLaughlin, M. J., & Croninger, R. G. (2007). Sociocultural correlates of disciplinary exclusion among students with emotional, behavioral, and learning disabilities in the SEELS national dataset. *Journal of Emotional and Behavioral Disorders, 15*(1), 33–45.

Alexander, M. (2012). *The new Jim Crow*. The New Press.

Allport, G. W. (1954). *The nature of prejudice*. Addison-Wesley

Alvarez, A. N., Liang, C. T., & Neville, H. A. (Eds.). (2016). *The cost of racism for people of color*. American Psychological Association.

Banaji, M. R., & Greenwald, A. G. (2013). *Blindspot: Hidden biases of good people*. Delacorte Press

Bartholomew, C. (1987). *The effect of dialect differences on the scoring of ambiguous WISC-R responses: An evaluation of scoring bias*. The Graduate School, University of Southern Mississippi

Brock, S. E. (2015, May 1). Mental health matters. *Communique, 43*(7), 13–15.

Burch, A. D. S., & Ploeg, L. V. (2022, May 16). Buffalo shooting highlights rise of hate crimes against black Americans. *The New York Times*. nytimes.com

Carter, P., Skiba, R., Arredondo, M., & Pollock, M. (2014). *You can't fix what you don't look at: Acknowledging race in addressing racial discipline disparities*. The Equity Project at Indiana University.

Cherry, K. (2019). How does implicit bias influence behavior? *Verywellmind*. www. verywellmind.com/

Epstein, R., Blake, J. J., & González, T. (2017). *Girlhood interrupted: The erasure of Black girls' childhood*. Social Science Research Network

Girvan, E. J., Gion, C., McIntosh, K., & Smolkowski, K. (2017). The relative contribution of subjective office referrals to racial disproportionality in school discipline. *School Psychology Quarterly, 32*, 392–404. https://doi.org/10.1037/spq0000178

Goff, P. A., Jackson, M. C., Allison, B., DiLeon, L., Culotta, C. M., & DiTomasso, N. A. (2014). The essence of innocence: Consequences of dehumanizing black boys. *Journal of Personality and Sociology Psychology*, 526–545. www.apa.org/pubs/journals/releases/psp-a0035663.pdf

Golash-Boza, T. M. (2019). *Race and racisms*. Oxford University Press.

Kalat, J. W. (2017). *Introduction to psychology*. Cengage Learning.

Kang-Brown, J., Trone, J., Fratello, J., & Daftary-Kapur, T. (2013). *A generation later: What we've learned about zero tolerance in schools*. Vera Institute of Justice, Center of Youth Justice.

Kendi, I. X. (2019). *How to be an antiracist*. One World.

Lincoln, C. E. (1984). *Race, religion, and the continuing American dilemma*. Hill and Wang.

Matthew, D. B. (2015). *Just medicine*. New York University Press.

McNulty-Eitle, T., & Eitle, D. J. (2004). Inequality, segregation, and the overrepresentation of African Americans in school suspension. *Sociological Perspectives*, 269–287.

Merino, Y., Adams, L., & Hall, W. J. (2018, June 1). Implicit bias and mental health professionals: Priorities and directions for research. *Psychiatry Online*. https://doi.org/10.1176/appi.ps.201700294

National Association of School Psychologists. (2017, November). Implicit bias: A foundation for school psychologists. *Communique'*, 32–33.

Pew Research Center. (2013, August 22). *King's dream remains an elusive goal; Many Americans see racial disparities*. Pew Research Center.

Rich-Shae, A. M., & Fox, J. A. (2014). Zero tolerance policies. In G. W. Muschert, S. Henry, N. L. Bracy, & A. A. Peguero (Eds.), *Responding to school violence: Confronting the Columbine effect* (pp. 89–104). Lynne Rienner.

Skiba, R. J., Michael, R. S., Nardo, A. C., & Peterson, R. L. (2000). *The color of discipline: Sources of racial and gender disproportionality in school punishment*. U.S. Department of Education. https://files.eric.ed.gov/fulltext/ED468512.pdf

Skiba, R. J., Michael, R. S., Nardo, A. C., & Peterson, R. L. (2002). The color of discipline: Sources of racial and gender disproportionality in school punishment. *The Urban Review, 34*(4), 317–342. https://doi.org/10.1023/A:1021320817372

Snowden, L. R. (2003, February). Bias in mental health assessment and intervention: Theory and evidence. *American Journal of Public Health, 93*(2), 239–243. https://doi.org/10.2105/ajph.93.2.239. PMID: 12554576; PMCID: PMC1447723.

Staats, C., Capatosto, K., Wright, R. A., & Jackson, V. W. (2016). *State of the science: Implicit bias revue, 2016 edition*. Kirwan Institute for the Study of Race and Ethnicity.

Sue, D. W., Alsaidi, S., Awad, M. N., Glaeser, E., Calle, C. Z., & Mendez, N. (2019). Disarming racial microaggressions: Microintervention strategies for targets, White allies, and bystanders. *American Psychologist, 74*(1), 128–142. https://doi.org/10.1037/amp0000296

U.S. Department of Education. (2022). School climate and discipline: Know the data. *Up to Date*. Retrieved January 22, 2022, from https://www2.ed.gov/p0licy/gen/gui/school-discipline/data.html

U.S. Department of Justice. (2022). 2020 Hate crime statistics. *Up To Date*. Retrieved July 8, 2022, from Hate Crime Statistics | HATECRIMES | Department of Justice

Van Ausdale, D., & Feagin, J. R. (2001). *The first R.: How children learn race and racism.* Rowman & Littlefield Publishers

Wechsler, D. (1974). *Wechsler intelligence scale for children-revised.* Psychological Corporation.

SECTION III
TRANSFORMATIVE PRACTICES

6

THE BIOPSYCHOSOCIAL APPROACH
TO BEHAVIORAL HEALTHCARE

The previous chapters reviewed the history of the school-to-prison (STPP) and explained how various adverse biological, psychological, and social factors increase a child's chances of entering the STPP. Historically, these biological, psychological, and social adversities have been viewed as separate risk factors, or not considered at all in the scientific literature, and in many cases treated that way clinically. These approaches limit the development of a truly comprehensive assessment, which can adversely impact client/patient care (Campbell & Rohrbaugh, 2006). This chapter examines why a comprehensive behavioral healthcare approach, using a biopsychosocial model, is more appropriate in identifying and treating children who are at risk for the STPP.

In 1977, Engel proposed the biopsychosocial model to disease as an alternative to the biomedical model, which viewed mental health conditions as physical disturbances in the brain. According to Engel, mental health conditions are the result of biological, psychological, and/or social factors interacting in complex ways. The biopsychosocial model systematically considers these biological, psychological, and social factors, and their complex interactions and influence on health, and tries to prevent, reduce their level of severity, or treat them. The biopsychosocial model also advances a comprehensive understanding of disease

DOI: 10.4324/9781003284383-9

and treatment and is derived from general systems theory, which proposes that each system affects and is affected by the other systems. The biological system emphasizes the anatomical, structural, and molecular substrates of disease and their effects on the client's/patient's biological functioning. The psychological system, on the other hand, addresses the contributions of developmental factors, motivation, and personality to the client/patient's experiences of and reactions to illness. Lastly, the social system examines the cultural, environmental, and familial influences on the expression of, as well as the client/patient's experiences of illness.

The Biopsychosocial Model: A Novel Approach to Behavioral Health Care

The biopsychosocial approach to mental health practice was presented as early as 1917 as part of the psychiatry curriculum at the Johns Hopkins School of Medicine (Meyer, 1917). It was not, however, fully articulated until Engel (1977) argued that restricting our views on patients' illnesses to having solely biological causes excludes important psychological and sociocultural factors. Engel offered a holistic alternative to the prevailing biomedical model that had dominated the medical community since the mid-20th century (Borrell-Carrió et al., 2004). Engel believed that behavioral healthcare professionals could no longer focus on mental health alone but also must address biopsychosocial functioning.

The biopsychosocial approach to behavioral health care has been described as a philosophy of clinical care, a practical clinical guide, and the clinical application of behavioral science and ethics to behavioral health needs. According to Borrell-Carrió et al. (2004), the biopsychosocial model is a philosophy of clinical care and a necessary contribution to the scientific clinical method because it is a way of understanding the client/patient's subjective experience. This model is also seen as an essential contributor to accurate diagnosis, health outcomes, and humane care, and it explains how suffering, disease, and illness are affected by multiple levels of organization, from societal to the molecular. For the clinician, Borrell-Carrió et al. proposed a biopsychosocial-oriented clinical practice whose "pillars" include self-awareness, active cultivation of trust, an emotional style that is characterized by empathetic curiosity, a reduction of bias, the formulation of a therapeutic relationship, and communication of clinical evidence to foster dialogue, not just mechanical application of protocol.

According to Melchert (2015), the biopsychosocial approach to behavioral health care involves the clinical application of both behavioral science and professional ethics to address behavioral health needs and promote biopsychosocial functioning. This approach to behavioral health care, he said, is committed to a scientific understanding of human psychology, which requires a comprehensive systemic framework that fundamentally recognizes the interactions between the biological, psychological, and sociocultural levels of natural organization. In his seminal book *Biopsychosocial Practice*, Melchert (2015) asserted that many of the traditional psychological theoretical orientations, such as psychodynamic or cognitive behavior therapy, were not designed to provide comprehensive explanations of human psychology that incorporate the interactions between the biological, psychological, and sociocultural influences on human psychology. In contrast, he said, the biopsychosocial model's more holistic perspective makes the biopsychosocial approach to behavioral health care the ideal conceptual framework for understanding these dynamic influences.

The biopsychosocial model is a novel approach to behavioral health care, especially when examining children who are at risk for entering the STPP. This model's goal is the identification of potential biological, psychological, and/or social risk factor(s). Although examining troubled children biopsychosocially is an innovative approach to addressing the STPP, this approach is based on the well-established public health model of prevention, as is the lethal global outbreak of the Coronavirus Pandemic (COVID-19), which the world is currently trying to eradicate. As is indicated in Chapter 8, prevention science is a well-researched strategy in psychology, and its benefits are clearly evident in the biomedical sciences as humans battle COVID-19. The importance of prevention is emphasized by the National Research Council and Institute of Medicine (2009) to reduce the prevalence and impact of behavioral health problems, but prevention science remains underutilized in psychology, and research is extremely limited. Prevention science emphasizes evidence-based practices, uses psychological or medical theory to advance health (at the individual and systemic levels) and well-being, works in partnership with other disciplines and specialties, and contributes to evidence-based interventions designed to prevent problems (Romano, 2015). In essence, the biopsychosocial approach to behavioral health care is designed to intervene when problems are first identified and is designed to prevent problems that could be reversed. This preventive aspect of the biopsychosocial approach is particularly appropriate for school-age children with mental, emotional, and behavioral (MEB) problems, so accurately identifying and possibly treating these youth is of enormous importance to themselves, their families, and to society in general.

Although the biopsychosocial approach to behavioral health care remains an ideal conceptual framework for understanding the dynamic influences on human psychology, has widespread use and acceptance throughout the physical health care and human services field, and retains widespread consensus across mental health specializations regarding the importance of integrating biological, psychological, and social factors into client/patient case conceptualizations, very little examination of its use in clinical psychological practice has been conducted. In psychological practice, there are many reliable and valid psychological assessments with extensive research credibility which can be used to evaluate one's social, emotional, behavioral, educational, intellectual, and personality functioning. Many of these assessments may be used as components in the biopsychosocial approach to behavioral healthcare to provide normative data and a broad picture of a client/patient's weaknesses and strengths, as well as his or her risks and protective factors. The biopsychosocial approach to case conceptualization, however, provides a more holistic perspective of these dynamic and complex psychological variables. The biopsychosocial approach helps the mental health provider(s) understand the potential positive or negative impact of a client's/patient's strengths and weaknesses, as well as his or her risks, protective factors, and resilience, so interventions can be targeted and specific to the individual's needs (Melchert, 2015).

Biopsychosocial versus Traditional Approaches

Unlike the biopsychosocial approach, traditional approaches to mental health education and practice often involve learning one or more of the well-accepted theoretical orientations, and then applying that approach to conceptualize clinical cases and deliver treatment. In the first half of the 20th century, American psychiatry strongly endorsed psychoanalytic approaches and, in the 1980s, a biological approach as well. Clinical psychology often adopted behavioral and cognitive approaches, but counseling psychology was heavily influenced by humanistic theories. Both social work and marriage and family therapy were influenced by systemic approaches and substance abuse approaches, and substance abuse treatment often used mutual aid support groups. Still today, one's adopted theoretical orientation has a major influence on case conceptualization and treatment. For example, if one ascribes to cognitive therapy, a client/patient's depression is likely to be conceptualized as being caused by irrational beliefs, and treatment would likely involve replacing those beliefs with more rational ones. On the other hand, if one ascribes to a biological psychiatry model of depression, one is likely to conceptualize the same depressive symptoms as resulting from a serotonin deficiency in the brain, and the treatment would likely include antidepressant medication (Melchert, 2015).

Melchert (2015) proposed that the biopsychosocial approach be used in behavioral health care because it builds on scientific knowledge regarding human development and functioning, and it integrates this knowledge into what is known about the whole person. From this perspective, he said, all research that explains psychological processes is valued, as are all therapies and other interventions that have been demonstrated to be safe and effective in relieving distress and improving biopsychosocial functioning.

Behavioral Health Care Assessment

The biopsychosocial approach to behavioral health care includes the use of a behavioral health care assessment, which is considered the first step in the assessment process. This assessment is also considered a part of treatment. Assessment procedures vary significantly, however, depending on the specific purpose or setting, such as a community mental health center, an independent specialty psychotherapy practice, or an educational setting (Melchert, 2015). In addition, the predominant mode of instruction in many contemporary training programs, such as psychiatry, nursing, psychology, and social work, has typically emphasized that the interviewer focuses predominantly, and in some cases exclusively, on one or at the most two of the three biopsychosocial components already identified. This approach limits the development of a comprehensive behavioral health care assessment and can impact client/patient care. Another confounding factor is that the behavioral health care assessment is also frequently given various names, such as Biopsychosocial Formulation (Campbell & Rohrbaugh, 2006), Biopsychosocial Assessment, and, of course, Behavioral Healthcare Assessment. This can be confusing to the novice examiner/interviewer since consensus about the name of this instrument and its components remains elusive. In this book, however, we refer to this instrument as the Comprehensive Behavioral Health Care Assessment for Children and Adolescents because of the relevance of its name to the population being discussed and the information being obtained.

The completion of the Comprehensive Behavioral Health Care Assessment for Children and Adolescents should occur continuously throughout treatment, if treatment is indicated, and is linked to the concept of either preventing problems or developing early intervention strategies to prevent long-term negative outcomes. This assessment is critical at the beginning of any formal mental health prevention or treatment process because it determines which areas of a client/patient's life need to be considered in developing comprehensive case conceptualizations or formulations to meet his or her biopsychosocial needs. This assessment also determines how or whether to proceed and if further intervention or contact is needed between the client/patient and mental health treatment provider (Melchert, 2015).

Although the procedures for conducting behavioral health care assessments may differ, when the various guidelines were reviewed and synthesized by Melchert in 2015, the following purposes of an assessment were revealed:

1. Identify behavioral health problems and concerns that require clinical attention.
2. Gather information regarding a patient's behavioral health and biopsychosocial functioning in order to develop a comprehensive case conceptualization and treatment plan.

3. Engage the client/patient in the treatment process through a collaborative approach that includes client/patient self-assessment and a discussion of objective feedback provided back to the patient.
4. Provide ongoing assessment during treatment in order to monitor progress, refine the treatment plan, and refocus interventions as needed.
5. Provide baseline data for an outcome's evaluation and assessment of the effectiveness of treatment.

Melchert concluded that these overarching basic purposes apply, even though the specific purposes of the assessment in particular cases vary (2015).

Behavioral Health Care Assessment and the DSM-5

According to Melchert (2015), over the last 50 years, behavioral health care assessment has gradually become more biopsychosocial in orientation, a change he sees as clearly reflected in the evolution of the Diagnostic and Statistical Manual of Mental Disorders (DSM). The DSM was first published in 1952 by the American Psychiatric Association, and the first two editions, DSM-I (American Psychiatric Association, 1952) and DSM-II (American Psychiatric Association, 1968), relied heavily on psychoanalytic theory. For many diagnoses, symptoms for specific disorders were seen as reflections of broad, underlying conflicts or reactions to life problems. The third edition used an atheoretical descriptive approach that did not specify or imply etiology for most disorders, but it introduced the multiaxial assessment system. This multiaxial system was used for three decades until the publication of DSM-5 in 2013 (American Psychiatric Association) and incorporated what is essentially a biopsychosocial approach to assessment. This approach includes clinical disorders on Axis I; personality disorders and pervasive developmental disorders on Axis II; medical issues on Axis III; environmental stressors on Axis IV; and general overall level of functioning on Axis V. In the DSM-5, Axes I, II, and III are combined, but separate notations are to be made for important psychosocial and environmental factors and disability. The DSM-5 also recommends the use of Z codes from the International Classification

Domain Component	Common Issues
	Biological Functioning
General Medical History	Current medical functioning, recent and past medical history, chronic medical conditions, physical disability, undiagnosed health complaints, previous hospitalizations, surgery history, seizure history, physical trauma history
Childhood Health History	Birth history, childhood illnesses, childhood psychiatric history
Medications	Dosage, efficacy, side effects, duration of treatment, medication adherence
Health Habits and Behaviors	Diet and nutrition, activity, exercise
	Psychological Functioning
History of Present Problem	Reason for seeking treatment at the present time, recent symptoms, exacerbations, or remissions of current illness or presenting problem, duration of current complaint, previous attempts to solve the problem, treatment readiness (e.g., motivation to change, ability to cooperate with treatment)
Level of Psychological Functioning	Overall mood and affect, level of distress, impairment in functioning
Individual Psychological History	Current psychiatric problems, previous diagnoses, treatment history (e.g., format, frequency, duration, response to treatment, satisfaction with treatment)
Substance Use and Addictions	Types of substances used (e.g., alcohol, tobacco, caffeine, prescribed, over the counter, illicit), quantity and frequency of use, previous treatments, other addictive behaviors (gaming, overeating, viewing pornography)
Suicidal ideation and risk assessment	Intent, plan, previous attempts, other self- and other-destructive behaviors (e.g., injury to self, neglect of self-care, homicidal risk, neglect of children or other dependents)
Individual Developmental History	Infancy, early and middle childhood, adolescence, early and middle adulthood, late adulthood
Childhood Abuse and Neglect History	Physical, sexual, emotional, psychological response to abuse or neglect
Other Psychological Traumas	Traumas and stressful life events, exposure to acts of war, political repression, criminal victimization

Figure 6.1 Biopsychosocial Component Areas of Behavioral Health Care Assessment

Note. From Foundations of Professional Psychology: The End of Theoretical Orientations and the Emergence of the Biopsychosocial Approach (pp. 124–125), by T. P. Melchert, 2011, London, England. Copyright by Elsevier.

Domain Component	Common Issues
Mental Status Examination	Orientation, attention, memory, thought process, thought content, speech, perception, insight, judgment, appearance, affect, mood, motor activity
Personality Style and Characteristics	Coping abilities, defense mechanisms, problem-solving abilities, self-concept, interpersonal characteristics, intrapersonal characteristics
Sociocultural Functioning	
Relationships and Support System	Immediate and extended family members, friends, supervisors, coworkers or other students, previous treatment providers, current parent-child relationship, involvements in social groups and organizations, marital-relationship status and history, recurrent difficulties in relationships, presence of past and current supportive relationships, sexual and reproductive history
Current Living Situation	Current living arrangements, satisfaction with those arrangements
Family History	Family constellation, circumstances, and atmosphere, recent problems with family, family medical illnesses, psychiatric history and diagnoses, history of suicide in first- and second-degree relatives, family problems with alcohol or drugs, loss of parent and response to that loss
Educational History	Highest level completed, professional or trade skills
Employment	Current employment, vocational history, reasons for job changes
Financial Resources	Finances and income
Legal Issues or Crime	Current legal issues and legal history, criminal victimization
Military History	Positions, periods of service, termination
Activities of Interest or Hobbies	Leisure interests and activities, hobbies
Religion	Organized religious practices and activities, active in faith
Spirituality	Personal beliefs, meaning, sense of purpose (which may or may not include a "higher power" or organized religious practices)
Multicultural Issues	Race-ethnicity, racial-ethnic heritage, country of origin, sexual orientation (i.e., lesbian, gay, bisexual, or transgender status), class

Figure 6.1 Continued

of Diseases to represent many of the problems individuals experience socially.

When conducting behavioral health care assessments, virtually all contemporary assessment systems indicate that it is important to include all three biopsychosocial domains, which include the biological, psychological, and sociocultural influences on human psychology. In 2011, Meyer and Melchert found substantial overlap when the specific areas included in six influential behavioral health assessment systems were compared. Twenty-six specific components were included in at least two of the systems, and 18 of the components were included in at least four of the systems. This overlap in these assessment systems suggested that all 26 of these component areas are important in the behavioral health care assessment. To evaluate the content-related validity of this set of assessment areas, Meyer and Melchert examined the information contained in 163 individual outpatient therapy files from three different clinics. They found that these 26 components captured 100% of the intake information found in the patient files. Melchert (2015) concluded that since each of these areas of a patient's life could be important in their development and current functioning, all of them needed to be considered when conducting behavioral health care assessments.

Meyer and Melchert (2011) did not provide a template of what a behavioral health care assessment should look like, but Melchert (2011) did provide a list of the 26 biopsychosocial component areas requiring assessment. These areas and components are listed in Figure 6.1 and have been incorporated into the Comprehensive Behavioral Health Care Assessment for Children and Adolescents, which is found in Chapter 7, along with instructions.

References

American Psychiatric Association. (1952). *Diagnostic and statistical manual of mental disorders*. American Psychiatric Association. https://ia800701.us.archive.org/10/items/dsm-1/dsm-1952.pdf

American Psychiatric Association. (1968). *Diagnostic and statistical manual of mental disorders* (2nd ed.). American Psychiatric Association. www.madinamerica.com/wp-content/uploads/2015/08/DSM-II.pdf

American Psychiatric Association, DSM-5 Task Force. (2013). *Diagnostic and statistical manual of mental disorders: DSM-5™* (5th ed.). American Psychiatric Publishing, Inc... https://doi.org/10.1176/appi.books.9780890425596

Borrell-Carrió, F., Suchman, A. L., & Epstein, R. M. (2004). The biopsychosocial model 25 years later: Principles, practice, and scientific inquiry. *Annals of Family Medicine, 2*(6), 576–582. https://doi.org/10.1370/afm.245

Campbell, W. H., & Rohrbaugh, R. M. (2006). *The biopsychosocial formulation manual.* Routledge. https://doi.org/10.4324/9780203956489

Engel, G. L. (1977). The need for a new medical model: A challenge for biomedicine. *Science, 196,* 129–136.

Melchert, T. P. (2011). *Foundations of professional psychology: The end of theoretical orientations and the emergence of the biopsychosocial approach.* Elsevier. https://doi.org/10.1016/C2010-0-66696-X

Melchert, T. P. (2015). *Biopsychosocial practice: A science-based framework for behavioral healthcare.* The American Psychological Association. www.apa.org/pubs/books/4317346.html

Meyer, A. (1917). Progress in teaching psychiatry. *Journal of the American Medical Association, 69,* 861–863. https://doi.org/10.1001/jama.2017.10486. PMID: 28898369.

Meyer, L., & Melchert, T. P. (2011). Examining the content of mental health intake assessments from a biopsychosocial perspective. *Journal of Psychotherapy Integration, 21*(1), 70–89. https://doi.org/10.1037/a0022907

The National Research Council and the Institute of Medicine. (2009). *Preventing mental, emotional, and behavioral disorders among young people: Progress and possibilities.* The National Academies Press. https://doi.org/10.17226/12480.

Romano, J. L. (2015). *Prevention psychology: Enhancing personal and social well-being.* The American Psychological Association. www.apa.org/pubs/books/4317347?tab=1

7

THE COMPREHENSIVE BEHAVIORAL
HEALTHCARE ASSESSMENT FOR CHILDREN
AND ADOLESCENTS

This chapter introduces the Comprehensive Behavioral Healthcare Assessment for Children and Adolescents, which uses the 26 biopsychosocial component areas identified by Melchert (2011) in the previous chapter. As is indicated in the previous chapter, the completion of the Comprehensive Behavioral Healthcare Assessment for Children and Adolescents is considered the first step in the assessment process and a part of treatment (if treatment is necessary). It is partially completed during referral but largely during the treatment process. Therefore, it is not recommended that this questionnaire be completed in its entirety when a child is first identified with mental, emotional, and/or behavioral health problems.

Chapters 9 and 10 provide more specifics about the completion of the Comprehensive Behavioral Healthcare Assessment for Children and Adolescents and explain who is best, if the child is a student, to facilitate this process. Of the five guidelines identified by Melchert (2015) in the previous chapter, only the first two guidelines may need to be addressed in this questionnaire if the child is being referred by a school staff member. These two guidelines include identifying behavioral health problems and concerns that require clinical attention and gathering information regarding a client/patient's behavioral health and biopsychosocial functioning in order to develop a comprehensive case conceptualization and

DOI: 10.4324/9781003284383-10

treatment plan. It should take about 30 minutes to complete these sections. Items addressing these guidelines that need completion are highlighted in a light gray color on the Comprehensive Behavioral Healthcare Assessment for Children and Adolescents. Most teachers are familiar with the questions asked in these sections because many similar ones are asked in the school when a child is being referred for special education consideration or behavioral health interventions. The last three guidelines should be addressed during treatment by a mental health provider.

Completing the Comprehensive Behavioral Healthcare Assessment for Children and Adolescents requires considerable collection of data across the three biopsychosocial functioning areas, which include the biological, psychological, and social areas. If the client/patient/student is a child, a large part of this instrument can be completed independently by the parent, guardian, or caretaker. If the child is adopted or in foster care, it may be necessary to obtain assistance in completing this questionnaire from the child's physician, juvenile justice worker, or social service agency personnel. As explained in Chapter 10, seeking the input of other professionals outside of the school system may be cumbersome and time-consuming, but this interaction is an opportunity to build a collaborative team and support system for addressing the youth's needs. If the Comprehensive Behavioral Healthcare Assessment for Children and Adolescents is completed by a teenager or young adult, a consultation with the parent may also be necessary to obtain information about this individual's early development.

Regardless of the child or adolescent's age, an affirmative response to some of the questions (e.g., experiences of abuse, suicidal thoughts/attempts) may require additional follow-up with more detailed and comprehensive questions. This is most likely to occur if an interviewer/examiner interviews a young child alone. Teachers and mental health practitioners have protocols they must follow if certain comments are made to them by children and adolescents. The benefit of a collaborative team, where there is access to other professionals (e.g., mental health, social services, etc.), is invaluable in these rare circumstances.

If an interviewer/examiner is involved with the completion of this questionnaire, he or she should have good interviewing and relationship-building skills so rapport can be developed, and reliable and accurate information collected. If the client/patient/student is a child, effective communication and collaboration skills are also needed to interact effectively with parents/caregivers and teachers who may believe that some of the questions are too personal. This can be assessed by asking the respondents about their comfort level when responding to certain questions. To mitigate respondents' anxiety or concern, they should be informed of the importance of an accurate and complete assessment of the child's biological, psychological, and social history so that strengths and weaknesses can be identified, along with risks and needs. It may also be helpful to remind the respondent that the information obtained is confidential and will not be shared with anyone who is not involved with this child's education and/or mental health treatment.

COMPREHENSIVE BEHAVIORAL HEALTHCARE ASSESSMENT FOR CHILDREN AND ADOLESCENTS

Dear Parent/Guardian/Caretaker/Client/Patient,

By completing this questionnaire, you acknowledge that it is not a diagnostic instrument and is for information purposes only.

Please Sign and Date:_____

Client/Patient Name:					
Client/Patient Race:					
Client/Patient Address:					
Phone Number:					
City:		State:		Zip:	
Date of Birth:		MM/DD/YY	Sex:	☐ Male ☐ Female ☐ Transgender ☐ Other	
Parent/Guardian's Name:					
Parent/Guardian's Address (if different from above):					
City:		State:	Zip:		

Contact Information (Secure consents for agency contacts, when possible.)

Name of Caseworker	Agency	Phone Number

Client/Patient/Parent/Teacher's (Circle One) Presentation of the Problem:
Client/Patient/Parent/Teacher's (Circle One) Expected Outcome:

CURRENT GENERAL MEDICAL HISTORY
OF CLIENT/PATIENT

Please complete the questions below. Enter additional details to explain yes responses.

	Yes	No	Explanation
Is there a history of medical problems?	☐	☐	
History of heart problems?	☐	☐	
An abnormal electrocardiogram (ECG or EKG)?	☐	☐	
Chronic, recurrent, or morning cough?	☐	☐	
Stomach or intestinal problems?	☐	☐	
Significant vision or hearing problems?	☐	☐	
(Girls Only) Menstrual period problems?	☐	☐	
	☐	☐	
	☐	☐	
Questions/Concerns:			

Date of last dental exam _____	☐ Normal ☐ Abnormal ☐ Can't Remember
Medications:	
List any current prescribed medications.	
List any self-prescribed medications, dietary supplements, vitamins.	
List any hospitalizations and or surgeries (reason).	

PAST MEDICAL HISTORY

Condition	Yes	No	Explanation
Heart attack	☐	☐	
Heart murmur	☐	☐	
Disease of arteries	☐	☐	
Arthritis	☐	☐	
Diabetes	☐	☐	
Epilepsy or seizures	☐	☐	
Stroke	☐	☐	
Anemia	☐	☐	
Thyroid problems	☐	☐	
Pneumonia	☐	☐	
Bronchitis	☐	☐	
Asthma	☐	☐	
Injuries	☐	☐	
Broken bones	☐	☐	
Jaundice or gallbladder problems	☐	☐	

HEALTH HABITS AND BEHAVIORS					
Have you ever smoked cigarettes, cigars, or a pipe?	☐ Yes ☐ No		How many per day? _____		
What do you consider a good weight for yourself?					
What is the most you have ever weighed?					
Current weight					
Number of meals consumed daily					
Number of glasses, cups, containers of the following:	☐ *milk* _____	☐ coffee	☐ tea _____	☐ regular/diet soda	☐ water _____
Do you drink alcoholic beverages?	☐ Yes ☐ No				
	Beer	☐ None ☐ Occasionally ☐ Often If so, _____ per week			
	Wine	☐ None ☐ Occasionally ☐ Often If so, _____ per week			
	Hard Liquor	☐ None ☐ Occasionally ☐ Often If so, _____ per week			

HISTORY OF PRESENT PROBLEM

Presenting problem (What brought you here today/Why is this Student being referred?)	
Onset of problem (When did problem begin?)	
Recent symptoms	
Duration of symptoms (How long have symptoms been present?)	_____ days _____ months _____ years
Why do you feel the need for services?	
Past treatments? ☐ Yes ☐ No	Facility _____ Contact _____

Stage of Change	☐ Precontemplation _____
	☐ Contemplation _____
	☐ Preparation _____
	☐ Action _____
	☐ Maintenance _____

PSYCHOLOGICAL HISTORY

Please check the following words you would use to describe yourself.			
☐ Intelligent	☐ Confident	☐ Worthwhile	☐ Ambitious
☐ Sensitive	☐ Loyal	☐ Trustworthy	☐ Evil
☐ Full of Regrets	☐ Worthless	☐ A Nobody	☐ Useless
☐ Crazy	☐ Deviant	☐ Unattractive	☐ Ugly
☐ Considerate	☐ Unlovable	☐ Inadequate	☐ Naive
☐ Confused	☐ Hardworking	☐ Incompetent	☐ Stupid
☐ Attractive	☐ Persevering	☐ In Conflict	☐ Honest
☐ Suicidal	☐ Can't Make Decisions	☐ Memory Problems	☐ Good Sense of Humor

Please check any of the following that apply to your childhood or adolescence.			
☐ Unhappy Childhood	☐ Family Problems	☐ School Problems	☐ Emotional/ Behavioral Problems
☐ Alcohol Use	☐ Drug Abuse	☐ Medical Problems	☐ Legal Problems
☐ Physical Abuse	☐ Sexual Abuse	☐ Emotional Abuse	☐ Other

Has client/patient ever been in counseling or psychotherapy?		
When:	*MM/DD/YY*	Where:
For how long:		For what:
Has client/patient taken medication for a psychological problem or mental disorder in the past? ☐ Yes ☐ No		
If yes, what medication?		
Dosage?		
When did client/patient begin medication?		
When did client/patient stop medication?		
What was it prescribed for?		

Has client/patient ever been hospitalized for psychological problems? ☐ Yes ☐ No
When?
Where?
Please explain:

Has client/patient ever attempted suicide? ☐ Yes ☐ No	How many times?	Age Attempted?
What method did client/patient use?		
Please explain:		

Has client/patient ever received a diagnosis of a mental, emotional, or behavioral health problem? ☐ Yes ☐ No		
When?	*What was the diagnosis?*	
How does client/patient feel about the diagnosis?		
Has client/patient ever had a psychological evaluation?		
When?	*Where?*	*Reasons:*
What were the recommendations?		

Does any member of client/patient's family suffer from depression or anything else that might be considered a psychological problem? ☐ Yes ☐ No
Has any member of client/patient's family ever been in counseling/therapy? ☐ Yes ☐ No
Has any member of client/patient's family ever been hospitalized for psychological problems? ☐ Yes ☐ No
Has any relative ever attempted or committed suicide? ☐ Yes ☐ No

SUBSTANCE ABUSE HISTORY

Drug Type	Age First Used	Age Heaviest Use	Recent Pattern of Use (frequency & amount)	Mode (1-oral, 2-smoking, 3-nasal, 4-injection)	Date of Last Use	Rank (1 least use, 5 most use)
Alcohol						
Cannabis						
Stimulants (crystal, speed, amphetamines, etc.)						
Inhalants (gas, paint, glue, etc.)						
Hallucinogens (LSD, PCP, mush-rooms, etc.)						
Opioids (heroin, narcotics, meth-adone, etc.)						
Sedative/Hyp-notics (Valium, etc.)						
Designer Drugs/ Other (herbal, steroids, cough syrup, etc.)						
Tobacco (smoke, chew)						
Caffeine						

Drug(s) of Choice:

Consequences as a Result of Drug/Alcohol Use (select all that apply):

☐ Hangovers	☐ DTs/Shakes	☐ Blackouts	☐ Binges
☐ Overdose	☐ Increased Tolerance	☐ GI Bleeding	☐ Liver Disease

☐ Sleep Problems	☐ Seizures	☐ Relationship Problems	☐ Left School
☐ Lost Job	☐ DUIs	☐ Assaults	☐ Arrests
☐ Jail	☐ Homicide	☐ Other:	
Longest period of sobriety?		How long ago?	

Triggers to use (list all that apply):	
Have you traded sex for drugs? ☐ No ☐ Yes, explain:	
Have you been tested for HIV? ☐ No ☐ Yes	
If yes, date of last test:	Results:
Risk Taking/Impulsive Behavior (current/past)—select all that apply:	

☐ Unprotected Sex	☐ Shoplifting	☐ Reckless Driving
☐ Gang Involvement	☐ Drug Dealing	☐ Carrying/Using Weapon
☐ Other (Please explain):		

SUICIDAL IDEATION AND RISK ASSESSMENT

In the past year, have you made any plans to harm yourself?	☐ No ☐ Yes If yes, please be specific about plans or methods:
Do you have history in self-harm, threats, suicidal ideation, or suicidal thoughts?	☐ No ☐ Yes If yes, please be specific about the plans or methods you have considered:
There is a big difference between having a thought and acting on a thought. Do you think you might actually attempt to harm yourself?	☐ No ☐ Yes If yes, please be specific about how you may proceed with this:
In the past month, have you told anyone that you may commit suicide, or threatened that you may do it?	☐ No ☐ Yes If yes, who did you tell and what did you say to this person:
Do you have access to your suicide plan?	☐ No ☐ Yes If yes, please provide detail (i.e., type of pills, access to guns, location):

Have any of your family members or close friends or acquaintances completed suicide or made serious attempts?	☐ No ☐ Yes If yes, please be specific (who, when, and how it was fulfilled):	
Mental/Introspective Thought	**Yes**	**No**
Client/patient believes that he/she is speaking honestly with him/herself.		
Client/patient looks at both problems & accomplishments as an indicator of his/her sense of self.		
Client/patient examines the ways in which he/she has tried to manipulate, control, or manage the lives of others.		
Client/patient acknowledges that changes in his/her life must start with him/her.		

INDIVIDUAL DEVELOPMENTAL HISTORY

During pregnancy, biological mother had (select all that apply):		
☐ Amniocentesis	☐ Anemia	☐ Diabetes Mellitus
☐ Emotional Problems	☐ Excessive Weight Gain	☐ German Measles
☐ High Blood Pressure	☐ High Fever	☐ Kidney Problems
☐ No Prenatal Care	☐ Placenta Previa	☐ Premature Labor
☐ Vaginal Bleeding	☐ Vaginal Infection	☐ Other Infection
☐ Unknown	☐ Other:	

During pregnancy, did the mother use any of the following (select all that apply):			
☐ Tobacco	☐ Alcohol	☐ Street Drugs	☐ Unknown

Comments (frequency and intensity of use, participation in treatment, birth defects or malformations due to drug/alcohol use among siblings):

List any problems with labor/delivery:

Apgar scores:

Did client/patient have any of the following after delivery (select all that apply):

☐ Anemia	☐ Apnea		☐ Birth Defects	☐ Blood Transfusions

☐ Brady-cardia	☐ Cord Around Neck		☐ Eye Problems	☐ Fever/Low Temperature
☐ Hernia	☐ Hydrocephalus		☐ Infection	☐ Intensive Care
☐ Intra-cranial Bleed	☐ Jitteriness		☐ Physical Injury	☐ Seizures
☐ Trouble Breathing	☐ Trouble Sucking		☐ 1 of Multiples (twin, etc.)	
☐ Use of Oxygen	☐ Ventilator		☐ Yellow Jaundice	☐ Other:

Developmental Milestones—please select any that the client/patient did late or is still having trouble with:

☐ Rolling Over	☐ Sitting	☐ Standing
☐ Walking	☐ Engaging Peers	☐ Toileting
☐ Dressing Self	☐ Feeding Self	☐ Sleeping Alone
☐ Tolerating Separation	☐ Playing Cooperatively	☐ Speaking

Are immunizations up to date? ☐ Yes ☐ No

CHILDHOOD ABUSE AND/OR NEGLECT HISTORY

Is there any history of neglect (emotional, nutritional, medical, educational) or exploitation?
☐ Yes ☐ No
If yes, please explain:

Has client/patient been abused at any time in the past or present by family, significant others, or anyone else?
☐ Yes ☐ No
If yes, please explain:

Type of Abuse	By Whom	Age (s)	Currently Occurring? Y/N
Verbal putdowns			
Being threatened			
Made to feel afraid			
Pushed			
Shoved			
Slapped			
Kicked			

Strangled			
Hit			
Forced or coerced into sexual activity			
Other			
Was it reported? ☐ Yes ☐ No	To whom:		
Outcome:			
Has client/patient ever witnessed abuse or family violence? ☐ Yes ☐ No If yes, please explain:			

OTHER PSYCHOLOGICAL TRAUMAS

Event	Happened to me	Witnessed it	Learned about it	Not sure	Not applicable
Natural disaster (for example, flood, hurricane, tornado, earthquake)					
Fire or explosion					

MENTAL STATUS EXAMINATION

CATEGORY	SELECTIONS						
APPEARANCE	☐ Well Groomed		☐ Unkempt	☐ Disheveled		☐ Malodorous	
BUILD	☐ Average		☐ Thin	☐ Overweight		☐ Obese	
DEMEANOR	☐ Cooperative		☐ Hostile	☐ Guarded		☐ Withdrawn	
	☐ Preoccupied			☐ Demanding	☐ Seductive		
EYE CONTACT	☐ Average			☐ Decreased	☐ Increased		
ACTIVITY	☐ Average			☐ Decreased	☐ Increased		
SPEECH	☐ Clear	☐ Slurred		☐ Rapid		☐ Slow	
	☐ Pressured	☐ Soft		☐ Loud		☐ Monotone	
	Describe:						
THOUGHT CONTENT							
DELUSIONS	☐ None Reported		☐ Grandiose		☐ Persecutory		☐ Somatic

	☐ Bizarre	☐ Nihilist	☐ Religious	
	Describe:			
OTHER	☐ None Reported	☐ Poverty of Content	☐ Obsessions	☐ Compulsions
	☐ Phobias	☐ Guilt	☐ Anhedonia	☐ Thought Insertion
	Describe:			

PERCEPTION

HALLUCINA-TIONS	☐ None Reportd	☐ Auditory	☐ Visual
	☐ Olfactory	☐ Gustatory	☐ Tactile
	Describe:		
OTHER	☐ None Reported	☐ Illusions	☐ Depersonalization	☐ Derealization

THOUGHT PROCESS

☐ LOGICAL	☐ Goal Oriented	☐ Circumstantial	☐ Tangential
☐ LOOSE	☐ Rapid Thoughts	☐ Incoherent	☐ Concrete
☐ BLOCKED	☐ Flight of Ideas	☐ Perseverative	☐ Derailment

DESCRIBE

MOOD

☐ EUTHYMIC	☐ Depressed	☐ Anxious
☐ ANGRY	☐ Euphoric	☐ Irritable

AFFECT

☐ FLAT	☐ Inappropriate	☐ Labile	☐ Blunted
☐ CONGRUENT WITH	☐ Full		☐ Constricted

BEHAVIOR

☐ NO BEHAVIOR ISSUES	☐ Assaultive	☐ Resistant
☐ AGGRESSIVE	☐ Agitated	☐ Hyperactive
☐ RESTLESS	☐ Sleepy	☐ Intrusive

MOVEMENT

☐ AKATHISIA	☐ Dystonia	☐ Tardive Dyskinesia	☐ Tics

DESCRIBE			
COGNITION			
IMPAIRMENT OF	☐ None Reported	☐ Orientation	☐ Memory
	☐ Attention/Concentration	☐ Ability to Abstract	
	Describe:		
INTELLIGENCE ESTIMATE	☐ Mental Retardation	☐ Borderline ☐ Average	☐ Above Average
IMPULSE CONTROL	☐ Good	☐ Poor	☐ Absent
INSIGHT	☐ Good	☐ Poor	☐ Absent
JUDGMENT	☐ Good	☐ Poor	☐ Absent

FAMILY HISTORY

Family's current and past psychiatric history:			
Please check all that apply during your childhood:	*Present entire childhood*	*Present part of childhood*	*Not present*
Mother	☐	☐	☐
Father	☐	☐	☐
Stepmother	☐	☐	☐
Stepfather	☐	☐	☐
Brother(s)	☐	☐	☐
Sister(s)	☐	☐	☐
Other:	☐	☐	☐

Describe Parents:	**Father**	**Mother**
Full Name:		
Occupation:		
Education:		
General Health:		

Parents' current marital status:	Yes	No	Details
Married to each other	☐	☐	
Separated	☐	☐	How long? ____years ____months
Divorced	☐	☐	How long? ____years ____months
Mother remarried	☐	☐	How many times?
Father remarried	☐	☐	How many times?
Mother involved with someone	☐	☐	
Father involved with someone	☐	☐	
Mother deceased	☐	☐	How long? ____ years ____ months Your age at death ____
Father deceased	☐	☐	How long? ____ years ____ months Your age at death ____

Is client/patient or was client/patient emancipated?	☐ Yes ☐ No
If so, please provide date and outcome:	
Please provide any special circumstances during childhood:	

RELATIONSHIPS AND SUPPORT SYSTEMS

Please provide detailed responses to the following:

Describe family relationships & desire for involvement in the treatment process:
Perceived level of support for treatment (scale 1–5 with 5 being the most supportive)?
Current and significant past social supports:
Significant relationships:
Spiritual supports/affiliations:

Current Living Situation

What are client/patient's current living arrangements?				
With whom does client/ patient live?				
List all persons in client/ patient's household:	Name	Age	Sex	Relationship to client/patient

Employment of Head of Household

	Check all that apply:	
☐	**Employed and satisfied**	
☐	**Employed but dissatisfied**	Explain:
☐	**Unemployed**	Details:
☐	**Co-worker conflicts**	Explain:
☐	**Supervisor conflicts**	Explain:
☐	**Unstable work history**	Explain:
☐	**Disabled**	Details:

Family Financial Resources

	Select all that apply:	
☐	No current financial problems	
☐	Large indebtedness	Explain:
☐	Poverty or below-poverty income	Details:
☐	Impulsive spending	Explain:
☐	Conflicts over finances	Explain:

Source of Family Income (select all that apply):			
Employed:		Unemployed:	Other:
☐ Seasonal	☐ Self-employed	☐ Actively Seeking Work	☐ Public Assistance
☐ Temporary	☐ Part-time	☐ Not Looking for Work	
☐ Full-time			

LEGAL ISSUES OF CLIENT/PATIENT

Past Or Current Legal Problems (select all that apply):		
☐ None	☐ Gangs	☐ DUI/DWI
☐ Arrests	☐ Conviction	☐ Detention
☐ Jail	☐ Probation	☐ Other:
If yes to any of the above, please explain:		
Any court-ordered treatment? ☐ Yes (explain below) ☐ No		
Ordered by:	Offense:	Length of Time:

MILITARY HISTORY OF CLIENT/PATIENT

☐ Involved with ROTC at School	

WHAT LIMITS CLIENT/PATIENT'S LEISURE/RECREATIONAL ACTIVITIES?

Which of the following do you participate in (select or insert all that apply)?			
Spend Time with Friends	☐	Sports/Exercise	☐
Classes	☐	Dancing	☐
Time with Family	☐	Hobbies	☐
Work Part-Time	☐	Watch Movies/TV	☐
Use Electronics (e.g., cell phone, etc.)	☐	Stay at Home	☐
Listen to Music	☐	Other:	☐
	☐		☐

RELIGION OF CLIENT/PATIENT

Please provide additional comments at the end of this section:	*Yes*	*No*
What kinds of religious beliefs are important to you and your family?	☐	☐
Do you feel part of a religious/spiritual community?	☐	☐
Do you have any favorite holidays/traditions/celebrations?	☐	☐
What religious practices do you follow?	☐	☐
Do you go to church?	☐	☐
Do you pray? What are your beliefs about prayer?	☐	☐
Additional Comments:		

Spirituality of client/patient	YES	NO
Does client/patient demonstrate a willingness to seek out new persons, places, and experiences?	☐	☐
Does client/patient have a desire to make a positive life change?	☐	☐
Does client/patient try to balance your rights, needs, and desires with those of others in order to achieve harmony?	☐	☐
Does client/patient desire personal harmony, balance, and freedom?	☐	☐
Does client/patient desire to strengthen their prayer life/belief system?	☐	☐
Additional comments:		
Knowledgeable about traditions, spirituality, or religion? Comment:	☐	☐
Practices traditions, spirituality, or religion? Comment:	☐	☐
How would you describe your spirituality?	☐	☐
Does client/patient see a traditional healer? Comment:	☐	☐

MULTICULTURAL ISSUES OF CLIENT/PATIENT

Please provide details of answers in the sections below:	Yes	No
Has client/patient ever been treated poorly because of his/her beliefs/ ethnicity/race, etc.?	☐	☐
What are some of the ways client/patient has been treated poorly?		
Has client/patient ever felt different from others because of client/patient's beliefs/ethnicity/race, etc.?	☐	☐
What are some of the ways the client/patient felt different?		
What are some wrong assumptions people have made about the client/patient or client/patient's family that have caused problems?		

References

Melchert, T. P. (2011). *Foundations of professional psychology: The end of theoretical orientations and the emergence of the biopsychosocial approach.* Elsevier. https://doi.org/10.1016/C2010-0-66696-X

Melchert, T. P. (2015). *Biopsychosocial practice: A science-based framework for behavioral healthcare.* The American Psychological Association. www.apa.org/pubs/books/4317346.html

SECTION IV

PREVENTION

A MORAL AND ETHICAL IMPERATIVE

8

THE PROMISE OF PREVENTION

This chapter examines the concept of prevention and the impact it has had on psychology. Particular attention is paid to preventing the school-to-prison pipeline (STPP), which, as noted earlier, is a complex problem. These complexities could possibly include a child's prior exposure to multiple risk factors, such as poverty, neglect, or violence. Prevention efforts can be difficult to implement because they may be obfuscated by entrenched personal and group biases or beliefs that have, as indicated earlier in this book, become systemic roadblocks in the climate and culture of many educational, mental health, social service, and juvenile justice institutions. Furthermore, many circumstances that could be ameliorated by prevention efforts may not be amenable to change, such as where a child lives (i.e., his or her environment) or his or her family's economic status (e.g., poverty). Despite these dismal biopsychosocial potential factors, however, there is a wealth of mental and behavioral health interventions that are preventive in nature and available for implementation in any situation if the problems associated with the STPP are approached with fidelity and from a public health perspective.

Prevention Psychology

Over the past few decades, there has been considerable discussion about preventing physical health problems like lung cancer, obesity, diabetes, and human immunodeficiency viruses (HIV), but what does prevention look like in psychology? This question was addressed by Romano (2015) in his book *Prevention Psychology, Enhancing Personal and Social Well-Being*. According to Romano, prevention emphasizes evidence-based practices that use psychological theory to advance health and well-being at the individual and systemic levels. Prevention also advocates for policies that promote institutional and societal change to enhance the health and well-being of a population. For Romano, prevention psychology works in partnership with other disciplines and specialties, and it contributes to evidence-based interventions designed to prevent problems and strengthen individual and community protections from personal and psychological distress (2015).

For many years, Caplan's (1964) definition of prevention was cited almost exclusively by professionals and provided an early and important framework for prevention in the mental health fields. This definition delineated three different types of prevention:

> Primary prevention—Interventions designed to prevent problems from occurring across the population or within a subgroup or system (e.g., comprehensive, school-based programs delivered to an entire school to prevent school violence and bullying).
>
> Secondary prevention—Efforts that target groups at risk for developing a problem (e.g., Head Start programs that provide preschool and early school education for low-income children identified as at risk for poor school achievement).
>
> Tertiary prevention—Efforts that focus on limiting the impact of a problem that has already occurred (e.g., early intervention programs for autistic children).

Cowen (1983) argued, however, that the tertiary component of Caplan's definition is actually more aligned with treatment than prevention. In response, Gordon (1987) offered three alternative prevention classifications:

> Universal prevention—Interventions similar to primary prevention interventions that offer value to an entire group or population (e.g., mass media messages that remind people to use seatbelts).

Selective prevention—Interventions that are most beneficial to individuals or subgroups with average or above-average risks for developing a disorder, or for individuals who may already be experiencing symptoms (e.g., summer academic curriculums for incoming college freshmen who did not meet traditional admission requirements).

Indicated prevention—Interventions for individuals or groups at high risk for an illness or problem behavior who may already be showing some symptoms of a problem at the subclinical level (e.g., programs that address alcohol use for high school students cited for underage drinking).

According to Romano (2015), both Caplan's and Cowen's prevention classifications have limitations because they were originally proposed for the prevention of physical health disorders and not the prevention of mental and behavioral health problems. Romano also believes that the traditional classifications are problematic because, in some settings and with some ages, it is difficult to determine who is at risk and who would benefit more from secondary, selective, or indicated preventive interventions. To expand the definition and conceptualization of prevention, Romano and Hage (2000) developed a new five-part definition that includes the following:

A. Stopping a problem from ever occurring, which is similar to primary and universal prevention.

B. Delaying the onset of an age-related problem (e.g., teen pregnancy) or intervening with those at risk for a problem, which is similar to secondary, selective, and indicated prevention.

C. Reducing the impact of an existing problem, which is similar to tertiary prevention.

D. Strengthening knowledge, attitudes, behaviors, and skills of individuals or groups to enhance protections against problems and disorders.

E. Supporting and advocating for institutional, community, and government policies that promote physical and emotional health and well-being.

Topics and perspectives included under Romano and Hage's (2000) prevention umbrella broadened even further to include the prevention and reduction of problems and behaviors of individuals and groups. The focus is no longer exclusively on the individual, client, or patient but also on those variables that place an individual at risk for problems and those that protect him or her against problems. Activities that promote systemic and institutional changes that enhance health and well-being are also considered and promoted as being very important to a comprehensive prevention program or strategy (Romano, 2015). An example of these systemic and institutional changes can be found in the definition of preventive interventions provided by The National Research Council and the Institute of Medicine's (2009) committee on the Prevention of Mental Disorders and Substance Abuse Among Children, Youth, and Young Adults. The definition includes those preventive interventions that occur before the onset of a problem and addresses the importance of risk and protective factors in the prevention or reduction of problem behaviors. In addition, advocacy and social justice efforts to promote equality, empowerment, and opportunity are now recognized as important prevention strategies that enhance lives and prevent disorders through systemic and institutional change (Vera & Kenny, 2013).

Prevention and the Public Health Model

Despite many barriers, psychological theories and perspectives with strong prevention components have been advancing since the second half of the 20th century and include a developmental model (Ivey et al., 2009), a multicultural framework (Sue et al., 1992), and a social justice orientation (Albee, 1986). In 2015, Romano wrote that the public health model is grounded squarely in science, has prevention as its primary purpose, and has a social justice perspective that views public health as a public good. This is critically important because individuals are likely to agree about the importance of public health and safety, but they often disagree about the means of achieving those types of goals.

Prior to the 1900s, the public health model focused almost exclusively on infectious diseases, but since then, its agenda and scope have evolved to encompass both behavior and lifestyle choices. The public health model now includes a highly diverse, interdisciplinary team, including physicians, nurses, dieticians, economists, political scientists, lawyers, sociologists, anthropologists, psychologists, social workers, engineers, and disability specialists, who are involved in discussions about any behavior and lifestyle choices that affect even the best-laid preventive efforts of the public health model. These professionals may not all hold public health degrees, but they bring a wealth of knowledge to the team. In 1959, the biologist Dubos observed that no major disease in the history of mankind had ever been conquered by therapists and rehabilitative modes alone. Ultimately, the cure was found through prevention. It is now an accepted fact that the dramatic improvements in human health over the past century and a half are not attributable exclusively to improvements in medicine but are also the result of a far larger role played by public health measures (Melchert, 2015).

Epidemiology, the basic science of public health practice (Rothman & Greenland, 1998), provides information about the prevalence and distribution of problems. It is where we get the term risk factor, which was invented in the 1950s when the Framingham Heart Study found that, rather than having a single cause, cardiovascular disease had many different contributing factors that increased the risk for disease (Melchert, 2015). These risk factors were identified as characteristics, variables, or hazards that, if present for a given individual, make it more likely that this individual, rather than someone selected from the general population, will develop a disorder (Institute of Medicine, 1994).

Risks and Protective Factors

Although it is evident from the data cited earlier in this publication that many of the risk factors associated with the school-to-prison pipeline (STPP) are not always amenable to change, they do highlight the complexity of this problem and provide insight into some of the things that can be done to lessen their impact. Much of this insight is obtained by looking at both risk and protective factors. According to Melchert (2015), risk and protective factors play critical roles in the development of dysfunction, disorders, developmental competence, and resilience. Protective factors are internal influences (e.g., psychological resilience, or the individual's ability to adapt to a stressful situation or adversity) or external influences (e.g., supportive parents or other adults within the community) that improve an individual's response to a risk factor (Rutter, 1979). Although research into the risk and protective factors for healthy and maladaptive development has been fragmented, Biglan et al. (2012) noted that the available research evidence supports these two conclusions:

1. Emotional and behavioral problems tend to co-occur, and these problems are largely from the same conditions.
2. To prevent multiple problems and increase the prevalence of young people who develop successfully, we must increase the prevalence of nurturing environments. These environments can be fostered by focusing on these four key features:
   (a) Biologically and socially toxic conditions, such as unhealthy diets, child abuse, and poverty, must be minimized because they interfere with healthy development.
   (b) Opportunities for young people to be involved in problematic behaviors must be limited through improved monitoring and appropriate enforcement of behavioral expectations and rules.
   (c) Prosociality, which is the motivation and skills needed to engage in prosocial roles in society, must be taught, promoted, and reinforced to increase mental, emotional, and behavioral well-being.
   (d) Psychological flexibility, which is being clear about our values and mindful of our thoughts and feelings, must be recognized as an important part of a healthy personality. In other words, individuals must be encouraged to act in the service of their values, even when their thoughts and feelings might discourage this.

The cumulative effect of risk and protective factors in predicting maladjustment is very powerful. However, according to Cicchetti and Rogosch (1996), the ability to predict what psychological outcomes will develop in particular individuals is imprecise, and many different developmental pathways may result in the same outcome (equifinality). Furthermore, one particular developmental starting point can lead to many different outcomes (multifinality).

According to Romano (2015) and Melchert (2015), prevention in the mental health profession, behavioral health care, and the behavioral sciences is at one of the most significant points in its development. The Patient Protection and Affordable Care Act, often shortened to the Affordable Care Act and nicknamed Obamacare, provides for prevention services that promote health and well-being and prevent diseases such as depression, sexually transmitted infections, and interpersonal violence. This law is the largest driver of change in the healthcare delivery system in the United States (Nordal, 2012).

In 1979, Rutter proposed that, as the number of risk factors that children face increases, the developmental status of the child decreases. Rutter's cumulative risk model showed that the following groups of children face an accumulation of risk factors that are associated with a variety of negative outcomes:

- Children with difficult temperaments
- Children with low intelligence
- Children who live in families with serious parental conflict
- Children who live in families where there is violence
- Children who live in families where there is substance abuse
- Children who live in families where there are behavioral disorders and
- Children who live in a distressed community with inadequate schools

These children may demonstrate impairment in multiple areas, including social interactions, problematic parent–child relationships, an inability to participate in childcare without expulsion, delayed school readiness, school problems, and physical health problems in adulthood (Kim-Cohen et al., 2005; Gaffrey et al., 2011). The clinical presentations can usually be distinguished from the social, emotional, and behavioral patterns of typically developing children by a child's symptoms, family history, and level of impairment (Wakschlaq et al., 2005), or by objective measures such as the screening of behaviorally at-risk children. The Comprehensive Behavioral Healthcare Assessment for Children and Adolescents can also be a useful tool in identifying many of the child's biopsychosocial problems.

Protective factors are equally important, even though their promotion has historically been given less attention in prevention work than the problem behaviors themselves (Romano, 2015). As is indicated earlier, protective factors are internal influences, such as psychological resilience or the individual's ability to adapt to adversity or a stressful situation, or external influences, such as supportive parents or other adults within the community, that improve an individual's response to a risk factor (Rutter, 1979). The importance of protective factors in prevention was recognized in the book *Preventing Mental, Emotional, and Behavioral Disorders Among Young People: Progress and Possibilities* (National Research Council and Institute of Medicine, 2009). In this publication, the Committee on the Prevention of Mental Disorders and Substance Abuse Among Children, Youth, and Young Adults added mental health promotion as a necessity for healthy development in the prevention of behavioral and mental disorders. Even though, according to this committee, mental health promotion is characterized by a focus on well-being rather than prevention of illness or disorder, its aim is to improve positive outcomes among young people and includes efforts to enhance individuals' ability to achieve developmentally appropriate tasks (developmental competence) and a positive sense of self-esteem, mastery, well-being, and social inclusion. It also aims to strengthen their ability to cope with adversity.

These conceptualizations of risk and protective factors are varied and highlight some of the complexities encountered when preventive interventions are considered. Some are easily implemented, but others require fundamental changes in the lives of individuals and the environments they call home, as well as thoughts and opinions of those individuals who identify and treat children with mental, emotional, and behavioral disorders. Of major importance, however, is the fact that they are based on years of scientific research, which makes them indispensable assets in the reduction and prevention of mental, emotional, and behavioral problems and mental, emotional, and behavioral disorders (MEB).

Multiple Factors Contribute to the Development of MEB Disorders

The good news, according to the National Research Council and Institute of Medicine (2009), is that research has identified multiple factors that contribute to the development of MEB disorders, and interventions have been developed to successfully intervene with these factors. Through the application of policies, programs, and practices aimed at eliminating risks and increasing strengths, it said, there is great potential to reduce the number of new cases of MEB disorders and significantly improve the lives of young people. This council concluded the following:

> A variety of factors—including individual competencies, family resources, school quality, and community-level characteristics— can increase or decrease the risk that a young person will develop an MEB disorder or related problem behaviors, such as early substance use, risky sexual behavior, or violence. These factors tend to have a cumulative effect: A greater number of risk factors (and for some, a longer exposure, such as from parental mental illness) increases the likelihood of negative outcomes, and a greater number of protective factors (e.g., resources within an individual, family strengths, access to mentors, and good education) decreases the likelihood of negative outcomes.

> This report makes the case that preventing the development of MEB disorders and related problems among young people, reducing risks, and promoting positive mental health should be high priorities for the nation.

> Families, policymakers, practitioners, and scientists share a conceptual commitment to the well-being of young people—that is not a new idea. However, a solid body of accumulated research now shows that it is possible to positively impact young people's lives and prevent many MEB disorders. In addition, a consensus is emerging around the need to promote positive aspects of emotional development. While additional research is needed, the efficacy of a wide range of preventive interventions has been established, particularly regarding those that reduce risk factors or enhance protective factors. Less research has been conducted to empirically evaluate strategies to implement relevant policies on prevention, to widely and effectively adopt preventive

interventions, to develop culturally relevant interventions, or to build the infrastructure for prevention so that effective practices are available to every family and young person who could benefit from them.

(pp. 16–17)

This is encouraging information by the National Research Council and Institute of Medicine, especially for those individuals who work and advocate for children who are at risk for entering the STPP (2009).

Proactive Screening of Behaviorally At-Risk Children

During the past two decades, considerable progress has been made in the proactive screening of behaviorally at-risk children who are on a trajectory to later destructive outcomes due to risk factor exposure and/or who present moderate to severe social and behavioral challenges to their teachers, peers, and sometimes primary caregivers (Loeber Farrington, & Mcglynn, 2000; Reid et al., 2002). However, best practices are not always followed. Knowing that moderate to severe emotional, behavioral, and relationship disorders are rarely transient and often have lasting effects, including measurable differences in brain functioning in school-aged children and a high risk of later mental health problems (Luby et al., 2009), is a compelling reason for the utilization of proactive screenings. There appears to be broad agreement that behavioral screening approaches should be cost efficient and accurate, display acceptable degrees of specificity and sensitivity, and incorporate multiple methods and informants. Unfortunately, these best practice characteristics are often absent in the routine screening efforts of many clinical settings (Severson et al., 2007). Additionally, as is indicated in Chapter 1 of this book, African American children who are sanctioned at school are less likely to have their misbehavior attributed to internal sources, such as depression or anxiety. Therefore, they are less likely to be considered appropriate screening candidates and more likely to enter the STPP. As was also indicated earlier, correctly identifying potential psychological causes could not only reduce the criminalization of behavior that is explained by underlying mental health concerns but could also encourage educators and clinicians to use different interventions (Cokley et al., 2014).

The Preventive Aspect of the Biopsychosocial Approach

As is noted in the previous chapters, the biopsychosocial approach to case conceptualization is the only viable option behavioral health science has that can provide a holistic perspective of the dynamic and complex psychological variables associated with the findings previously outlined about risks and protective factors. These findings allow mental health providers to understand the potential positive or negative impacts of an individual's strengths and weaknesses, as well as risks and protective factors, so interventions can be targeted and specific. The biopsychosocial approach to behavioral health care includes assessment, treatment planning, and treatment for those individuals with well-established social, emotional, and behavioral health needs. This process also focuses on the goals outlined in the public health model of prevention, which include stopping a problem from ever developing; delaying its onset; reducing its impact; strengthening the knowledge, attitudes, behaviors, and skills of individuals and groups to enhance protections; and supporting and advocating for institutional, community, and government policies that promote physical and emotional well-being. All these goals are essential in a well-developed prevention strategy.

As is also evident from the risks and protective factors outlined previously and the public health model of prevention, prevention efforts typically require a collaborative effort. Teachers, parents, peers, school administrators, community leaders, legislators, and other adults also have a vital role in creating the environments that either foster or suppress the emergence of many children and adolescents' problems (Sheridan & Gutkin, 2000). However, a dismal analysis of many of these environments was provided by Garbarino when he wrote that the mere act of living in society today is dangerous to the health and well-being of children and adolescents, and their social world has become poisonous to their development. It is uncertain if Garbarino's assessment of the dangers children and adolescents face is correct, but if one looks at, for example, the current pressing problem of gun violence in the United States, there is compelling evidence that he is (1995). According to the Children's Defense Fund, 3,410 children and teens were killed with guns in 2017, the greatest number since 1998, and another 18,201 children and teens were injured by gunfire (2019).

Prevention Requires a Paradigm Shift

The biopsychosocial approach to behavioral health care is focused on prevention. Prevention, however, is a challenge in the mental health community. The mental health community has been criticized because its words about prevention have been much more abundant than its actions (Romano, 2015). As stated earlier, although psychological theories and perspectives with strong prevention components were advanced in the second half of the 20th century, these theories and models are not taught with regularity in many applied counseling and psychology training programs (Conyne et al., 2008; Romano, 2015). In addition, although prevention is widely valued and appreciated, the field also suffers from having no large natural advocacy constituency, and the main beneficiaries of many preventive interventions are very young or have not yet been born (Melchert, 2015).

In 2009, the National Research Council and Institute of Medicine said that several core concepts underlie the ability to adopt prevention and promotion as priorities. The council views these concepts as essential elements that must be embraced by families, policy makers, service systems, and scientists in order to continue to make progress in this area. One very important core concept that underlies much of the content of this book is the need for a paradigm shift. Regarding a paradigm shift, the National Research Council and Institute of Medicine wrote the following:

> Prevention requires a paradigm shift. Prevention of MEB disorders inherently involves a way of thinking that goes beyond the traditional disease model in which one waits for an illness to occur and then provides evidence-based treatment. Prevention focuses on the question "What will be good for the child 5, 10, or more years from now?" and tries to mobilize resources to put these things in place. A growing body of prevention research points to the need for the national dialogue on mental health and substance abuse issues to embrace the healthy development of young people and, at the same time, to respond early and effectively to the needs of those with MEB disorders.
>
> (2009, p. 17)

The term paradigm shift was popularized by Kuhn (1962) in his book *The Structure of Scientific Revolutions*. Kuhn challenged long-standing beliefs about scientific progress, arguing that transformative ideas do not arise from the day-to-day, gradual process of experimentation and data accumulation. Instead, he said, revolutions in science occur when they disrupt accepted thinking and offer unanticipated ideas. Before a paradigm shift can be achieved in any field of science, he proposed, it is necessary to highlight and articulate the extant or enduring anomalies that cannot be addressed satisfactorily by current approaches. Today, these extant anomalies can be seen in the small percentage (24%) of youth with mental, emotional, and behavioral health disorders who receive treatment, a gap that is even greater for African Americans in comparison with White Americans (National Research Council and Institute of Medicine, 2009) and the custody rate of youth in the United States.

References

Albee, G. W. (1986). Toward a just society: Lessons from observations on the primary prevention of psychopathology. *American Psychologist, 41*(8), 891–898. https://doi.org/10.1037/0003-066X.41.8.891

Biglan, A., Flay, B. R., Embry, D. D., & Sandler, I. N. (2012). The critical role of nurturing environments for promoting human well-being. *The American Psychologist, 67*(4), 257–271. https://doi.org/10.1037/a0026796

Caplan, G. (1964). *Principles of preventive psychiatry*. Basic Books.

Children's Defense Fund. (2019). *Protect children not guns*. www.childrensdefense.org/wp-content/uploads/2019/09/Protect-Children-Not-Guns-2019.pdf

Cicchetti, D., & Rogosch, F. A. (1996). Equifinality and multifinality in developmental psychopathology. *Development and Psychopathology, 8*(4), 597–600. https://doi.org/10.1017/S0954579400007318

Cokley, K., Cody, B., Smith, L., Bealey, S., Miller, I. S. K., Hurst, A., Awosogba, O., Stone, S., & Jackson, S. (2014). Bridge over troubled waters. *Phi Delta Kappan, 96*(4), 40–45.

Conyne, R. K., Newmeyer, M. D., Kenny, M., Romano, J. L., & Matthews, C. R. (2008). Two key strategies for teaching prevention: Specialized course and infusion. *The Journal of Primary Prevention, 29*(5), 375–401. https://doi.org/10.1007/s10935-008-0146-8

Cowen, E. L. (1983). Primary prevention in mental health: Past, present, and future. In R. D. Felner, L. A. Jason, J. N. Moritsugu, & S. S. Farber (Eds.), *Preventive psychology: Theory, research, and practice* (pp. 11–25). Pergamon.

Dubos, R. (1959). *Mirage of health*. Harper and Row.

Gaffrey, M. S., Luby, J. L., Belden, A. C., Hirshberg, J. S., Volsch, J., & Barch, D. M. (2011). Association between depression severity and amygdala reactivity during sad face viewing in depressed preschoolers: An fMRI study. *Journal of Affective Disorders, 129*(1–3), 364–370. https://doi.org/10.1016/j.jad.2010.08.031

Garbarino, J. (1995). *Raising children in a socially toxic environment*. Jossey-Bass.

Gordon, R. (1987). An operational definition of disease prevention. In J. A. Sternberg & M. M. Silverman (Eds.), *Preventing mental disorders* (pp. 20–26). U. S. Department of Health and Human Services.

Institute of Medicine. (1994). *Reducing risks for mental disorders: Frontiers for preventive intervention research.* National Academy Press.

Ivey, A. E., Ivey, M. B., & Zalaquett, C. P. (2009). *International interviewing and counseling: Facilitating client development in a multicultural society.* Brooks/Cole.

Kim-Cohen, J., Arseneault, L., Caspi, A., Tomás, M. P., Taylor, A., & Moffitt, T. E. (2005, June). Validity of DSM-IV conduct disorder in 41/2–5-year-old children: A longitudinal epidemiological study. *American Journal of Psychiatry, 162*(6), 1108–1117. https://doi.org/10.1176/appi.ajp.162.6.1108. PMID: 15930059.

Kuhn, T. S. (1962). *The structure of scientific revolutions.* University of Chicago Press.

Loeber, R., Farrington, D. P., & Mcglynn, M. M. (2000). Serious and violent juvenile offenders: Risk factors and successful interventions. *Behavioral Disorders, 25*(4), 374–375. https://doi.org/10.1177/019874290002500406

Luby, J. L., Belden, A. C., Pautsch, J., Si, X., & Spitznagel, E. L. (2009). The clinical significance of preschool depression: Impairment in functioning and clinical markers of the disorder. *Journal of Affective Disorders, 112*(1–3), 111–119.

Melchert, T. P. (2015). *Biopsychosocial practice: A science-based framework for behavioral healthcare.* The American Psychological Association. www.apa.org/pubs/books/4317346.html

The National Research Council and the Institute of Medicine. (2009). *Preventing mental, emotional, and behavioral disorders among young people: Progress and possibilities.* The National Academies Press. https://doi.org/10.17226/12480.

Nordal, K. C. (2012). Healthcare reform: Implications for independent practice. *Professional Psychology: Research and Practice, 43*(6), 535–544. https://doi.org/10.1037/a0029603

Reid, J. B., Patterson, G. R., & Snyder, J. (Eds.). (2002). *Antisocial behavior in children and adolescents: A developmental analysis and model for intervention.* American Psychological Association. https://doi.org/10.1037/10468-000

Romano, J. L. (2015). *Prevention psychology: Enhancing personal and social well-being.* American Psychological Association

Romano, J. L., & Hage, S. M. (2000). Prevention and counseling psychology: Revitalizing commitments for the 21st century. *The Counseling Psychologist, 28*(6), 733–763. https://doi.org/10.1177/0011000000286001

Rothman, K., & Greenland, S. (1998). *Modern epidemiology* (2nd ed.). Lippincott Williams & Wilkins.

Rutter, M. (1979, July). Protective factors in children's responses to stress and disadvantage. *Annals of the Academy of Medicine,* Singapore, *8*(3), 324–338. PMID: 547874.

Severson, H. H., Walker, H. M., Hope-Doolittle, J., Kratochwill, T. R., & Gresham, F. M. (2007). Proactive, early screening to detect behaviorally at-risk students: Issues, approaches, emerging innovations, and professional practices. *Journal of School Psychology, 45,* 193–223. http://dx.doi.org/10.1016/j.jsp.2006.11.003

Sheridan, S. M., & Gutkin, T. B. (2000). The ecology of school psychology: Examining and changing our paradigm for the 21st century. *School Psychology Review, 29*(4), 485–502. https://doi.org/10.1080/02796015.2000.12086032

Sue, D. W., Arredondo, P., & McDavis, R. J. (1992). Multicultural counseling competencies and standards: A call to the profession. *Journal of Counseling & Development, 70*(4), 477–486. https://doi.org/10.1002/j.1556-6676.1992.tb01642.x

Vera, E. M., & Kenny, M. E. (2013). *Social justice and culturally relevant prevention.* SAGE Publications, Inc. https://dx.doi.org/10.4135/9781452275598

Wakschlag, L. S., Leventhal, B. L., Briggs-Gowan, M. J., Danis, B., Keenan, K., Hill, C., Egger, H. L., Cicchetti, D., & Carter, A. S. (2005). Defining the "disruptive" in preschool behavior: What diagnostic observation can teach us. *Clinical Child and Family Psychology Review, 8*(3), 183–201. https://doi.org/10.1007/s10567-005-6664-5

9

THE PUBLIC SCHOOL—THE FRONT LINE OF PREVENTION

For students in need of mental health interventions, the public school system has a history of providing mental, emotional, and behavioral health supports, while also offering an array of quality educational services. As is indicated in Chapter 3, adverse school-level practices exist, but the public school remains the logical place to implement preventive interventions for school-age children. This institution's role in prevention has been articulated repeatedly by researchers and academicians such as Burns et al. (1995), Sander (2010), Romano (2015), and Brock (2015) who identify the public school system as the front line of prevention, the most common entry point to mental health services, and the de facto mental health system for youth with mental health needs. In the *Handbook of Evidence-Based Practices for Emotional and Behavioral Disorders*, Seeley et al. (2014) describe schools as the ideal context to identify students in need of specialized mental health interventions and provide remedial services to promote success in an educational setting.

Every Student Succeeds Act

In response to the prevalence of mental, emotional, and behavioral (MEB) health problems among school-age children, federal policies have been developed to integrate mental health and education services into schools

DOI: 10.4324/9781003284383-13

(Evans et al., 2014). One of the most recent efforts has been the passage of the Every Student Succeeds Act (ESSA). The Every Student Succeeds Act replaced the No Child Left Behind Act (NCLB) and was signed into law by President Obama on December 10, 2015. A key goal of ESSA is to improve equity in education. As is indicated in Chapter 3, property taxes pay for nearly half of the funding of public schools, which creates large differences in funding between wealthy and impoverished communities (Biddle & Berliner, 2002). This equity gap generates large disparities in the presence of auxiliary professionals, such as tutors, school psychologists, counselors, social workers, and other support staff members. Poor school systems typically have greater need for the support of these professionals, but their absence locks many students who could benefit from their support into solving problems themselves, putting them at greater risk for entering the school-to-prison pipeline (STPP). Because this Act affords states more flexibility in setting their own respective standards for measuring school and student performance, each state gets to decide how it will improve student outcomes. In 2017, when states submitted their education plans to the Department of Education, some chose to focus on equity in teacher quality across certain groups of students, while others chose to focus on creating equitable school climates. Still others noted that they planned to first identify equity gaps and then develop plans to address these gaps (Strobach, 2018).

The Every Student Succeeds Act also allows those schools in need of improvement to choose from a range of school improvement activities if there is reasonable evidence that the efforts support improved student outcomes. In addition, it permits coordinated, comprehensive, mental, and behavioral health services and community–school partnerships when they are to be used as school-turnaround strategies. For students with MEB disorders, this is extremely important because ESSA authorizes states to use Title I, Title II, and Title IV funding streams, as well as funds reserved for schools identified for targeted support and improvement, to expand access to comprehensive school mental health services. This access was highlighted by Kelly Strobach when she wrote that mental and behavioral health services are essential components of comprehensive learning supports, and students' mental and behavioral health underlies every aspect of learning (2018).

There are, however, challenges in the analysis and implementation of any new programs in schools, even if they are developed at the district level. As is indicated in Chapter 3 of this book, public schools and the field of education operate as bureaucratic structures in the United States that do not adapt to unique and diverse environmental demands. In other words, macro-level systems may be put into place without taking into consideration the diverse characteristics at the micro-level, such as individual schools, communities, and families. This "institutional isomorphism," as Clark and Dockweiler (2020) described it, may not be driven with a goal toward organizational efficiency or use of best practices, but by coercive, mimetic, and normative processes. This example was provided:

> Schools are increasingly having demands placed on them from the outside, which hinders their ability and initiative to adapt and be reflective. Conversely, districts repeatedly have mandates put on them from the state forcing them to align with some standard, thus making both districts and schools more homogeneous. When these external forces have the power to dictate the narrative and the mandates, decision-making at the lower levels is compromised. According to neo-institutional policy research, organizations may increasingly be concerned with the goals of power rather than efficiency and, arguably, best practice.
>
> (p. 31)

In the school setting, this isomorphism and lack of adaptive responsiveness pose new challenges for school leaders, which may be mitigated by the adoption of the Multi-Tiered System of Supports (MTSS). The MTSS is a system of targeted support for students struggling academically or behaviorally. The MTSS framework can be represented by the overlapping, nonnegotiable variables of leadership, inclusiveness, quality control, universality, implementation and feedback looping, and data-based decision making (LIQUID). Each of these variables must be infused into all aspects of the framework to ensure success of the MTSS at a school and is the standard in which to compare all phases of the MTSS process (Clark & Dockweiler, 2020).

Schoolwide Positive Behavior Interventions and Supports

For all children, especially those with MEB health disorders, expanding access to comprehensive school mental health services through prevention and intervention options can be addressed by the use of schoolwide positive behavior interventions and supports (SWPBIS), which is currently being implemented in many schools throughout this country. As alluded to in Chapter 3, the typical practice in many schools is to develop a "get-tough" or "zero tolerance" approach to disciplining students who exhibit problematic behaviors (Sugai & Horner, 2006). To address behavioral infractions, the traditional school discipline ladder usually relies on the use of repeated warnings, reprimands, loss of privileges, corporal punishment, in-school and after-school detention, in-school and out-of-school suspension, and expulsion. These approaches are highly reactive in nature and operate under the flawed assumption that the student will learn the proper ways of behaving in order to avoid the consequences (Doggett et al., 2008). Research has revealed, however, that such approaches are ineffective for students displaying chronic behavioral concerns and often exacerbate the display of antisocial behavior in these students (Lewis et al., 1998).

This book is not advocating for the complete removal of traditional strategies used to discipline students who exhibit problematic behaviors that disrupt learning, especially if these discipline strategies are effective and do not contribute to the disproportionate entrance of African Americans and other children of color into the school-to-prison pipeline (STPP); instead, it encourages schools to use more proactive, comprehensive strategies designed to teach prosocial behavior. Schoolwide positive behavior interventions and supports is a proactive model that can do this. Schoolwide positive behavior interventions and supports is best defined as a decision-making framework that guides the selection, integration, and implementation of evidence-based academic and behavioral practices that can improve academic and behavior outcomes for all students (Evans et al., 2014). This model is an extension of positive behavior and supports (PBS), which is an applied science that uses empirically based methods to redesign important environments in an individual's life in order to expand their behavioral repertoire (Carr et al., 1999).

According to Domitrovich et al. (2010), SWPBIS is an MTSS prevention framework or model that has had considerable influence over the field of education for the past decade. The SWPBIS is designed to help educators and administrators organize their services, manage the flow of students across services, and evaluate and revise services according to students' needs. This framework is highly collaborative in nature, and its aims are to build the capacity of schools, families, and communities to (1) effectively teach and promote positive behaviors, academic achievement, and life skills; (2) reduce the prevalence and severity of problem behaviors; and (3) identify and provide evidence-based services to all students with particular needs. According to Evans et al. (2014), SWPBIS advances both the science and practice of school mental health because it provides an infrastructure and decision-making process for evidence-based services. If addressed with fidelity, the implementation of SWPBIS in the public school system can also address some of the adverse school-level practices mentioned in Chapter 4, such as the unmet needs of youth with mental, emotional, and behavioral health disorders, and explicit and implicit bias.

Overlap Between SWPBIS and the Public Health's View of Prevention

Positive behavior intervention and supports in the school system typically utilizes a three-tiered, needs-based approach to prevention and service delivery. Tier 1 provides positive behavioral support systems to all students as a form of primary prevention. Ideally, this tier is manifested as a pervasive shift in school culture because it teaches, recognizes, and praises positive behavior while deemphasizing and socially rejecting problematic behaviors. Tier 2 is designed for students who are not responsive to Tier 1 preventive interventions and provides more targeted support systems to at-risk groups. This prevention effort aims to reduce the number of existing problem behavior cases and prevent or decrease individual needs for Tier 3 services. Tier 3 interventions provide highly individualized and specialized support systems for high-risk students, with the goal of reducing the severity and intensity of individual problem behaviors. The SWPBIS model includes teams of professionals involved in the decision-making process that support and manage the provision of these services within a school.

SWPBIS is a tiered prevention model that emphasizes data-based decision making, progress monitoring, evidence-based interventions, collaboration, and monitoring of implementation fidelity. Therefore, there is considerable overlap in SWPBIS's three-tiered, needs-based approach to prevention and service delivery and Romano and Hage's (2000) public health view of prevention. As is indicated in Chapter 8, Romano and Hage proposed a five-part definition of prevention. The first part includes stopping a problem from ever occurring, which SWPBIS addresses through Tier 1. As is described earlier, Tier 1 provides positive behavioral support systems to all students as a form of primary prevention. The next step in the prevention paradigm is delaying the onset of an age-related problem, or intervening with those at risk for a problem, which is consistent with Tier 2 of SWPBIS. As previously indicated, this tier emphasizes targeted support systems for at-risk groups or simple individual plans for students who have not sufficiently responded to Tier 1 services. The next step of Romano and Hage's (2000) public health's view of prevention includes the reduction of the impact of an existing problem. This is consistent with Tier 3, where highly individualized and specialized support systems for high-risk students are implemented. At this point, teams of professionals are involved in the decision-making process that supports and manages the provision of services, with the understanding that collaboration with individuals and groups outside of the school system may be necessary.

Collaboration

As was indicated, the SWPBIS's decision-making framework is highly collaborative in nature and aims to build the capacity of schools, families, and communities to teach and promote positive behaviors, academic achievement, and life skills; reduce the prevalence and severity of problem behaviors; and identify and provide evidence-based services to all students with particular needs. All of these evidence-based services may not be accessible in the schools, but through collaborative services that are offered within the community.

The importance of collaboration can be seen in an article written by McDaniel (2016), former president of the American Psychological Association:

In most ways, Americans are highly individualistic. We believe our achievements are of our making (yet, somehow, our failures are often due to others). Our society and culture often shun the efficiencies and support of a group approach in favor of independence . . . .

But the American ideal of independence at-all-costs may have run its course in many arenas. In business in the latter part of the 20th century, U.S. automobile companies realized that the teamwork approach of Japanese car companies seemed to help them make better, more efficient and longer lasting cars more quickly than their American counterparts. In addition, studies began to show that errors in aviation and health care were often linked to traditional hierarchies that shut down communication from anyone but the leader. Teams with diverse membership, flattened hierarchies and rich communication were more likely to have positive outcomes.

Primary care itself is undergoing a transformation from a practice headed by a physician to care rendered by an interprofessional team. The complexities of health and illness mandate team-based over solo care with multiple people targeting the multiple aspects of a chronic illness—a physician who diagnoses and treats acute symptoms; a nurse who administers immunizations, draws blood and checks labs; a pharmacist, a nutritionist or a care manager who connects that patient with social agencies and other health professionals; and a psychologist or other behavioral health professional who consults on the meaning of the illness to the patient and family, their emotional reactions to it, desirable health behavior changes and much more.

(p. 4)

If manufacturing companies that produce inanimate objects realize the benefits of a group or collaborative approach, certainly there is merit in the use of interprofessional or collaborative teams when addressing the complex needs of students with mental, emotional, and behavioral disorders!

Despite the benefits of SWPBIS's highly collaborative framework, however, it is still important to maintain the privacy of protected health information when there is interaction between individuals, professional groups, schools, and mental health practitioners. This includes information that may identify a student, client, or patient that relates to his or her past, present, or future physical or mental health condition and related healthcare services. The Health Insurance Portability and Accountability Act of 1996 (HIPAA) is a federal law that requires the creation of national standards to protect sensitive patient health information from being disclosed without the patient's consent or knowledge. This Act ensures that individual healthcare plans are accessible, portable, and renewable, but it sets the standards and the methods for how medical data is shared across the U.S. health system. The U.S. Department of Health and Human Services (HHS) issued the HIPAA Privacy Rule to implement the requirements of HIPAA. The Privacy Rule standards address the use and disclosure of individuals' health information, known as protected health information, by entities subject to the Privacy Rule. The Privacy Rule also contains standards for individuals' rights, including those of school-age children, to understand and control how their health information is used. A major goal of the Privacy Rule is to ensure that individuals' health information is properly protected while allowing the flow of health information needed to provide high-quality health care and protect the public's health and well-being (Centers for Disease Control and Prevention, 2018).

SWPBIS, Collaboration, and Schools

As is indicated in the foregoing, the SWPBIS framework is highly collaborative in nature, and its aims are to build the capacity of schools, families, and communities. Children who enter Tier 3 of SWPBIS are often known to multiple organizations, such as mental health agencies, child protective services, and juvenile courts. All of these organizations have a vested interest in these children's health and welfare, but many operate as independent silos. Current research suggests that these organizations would be more effective if they worked together (Gross et al., 2017; Weist et al., 2018; Eber et al., 2014).

There are, however, challenges to organizations' ability to work together with schools, largely because public school systems typically do not consider themselves a component of a collaborative, even though SWP-BIS supports this alignment. Several factors have hampered progress in this area, including the distinct missions of schools and healthcare systems, as well as the lack of agreement on a clear, operational definition of collaboration across disciplines. Studies regarding collaboration are found across fields as diverse as health care, program evaluation and management, psychology, and communication, but a bewildering range of terms, constructs, and theories are applied to the notion of working together (Pollard et al., 2014). In addition, psychology researchers may interchangeably use terms such as coexistence, co-location, cooperation, partnering, networking, coordination, team building, coalition building, or collaboration, making study comparison difficult within their own discipline, much less outside of it (Doherty, 1995).

To address public schools' need to consider themselves a component of a collaborative, especially when working with troubled children at Tier 3 and/or those at risk for entering the school-to-prison pipeline, it should be kept in mind that collaboration of care exists on a continuum with levels that are qualitatively distinct from one another. Levels are differentiated by where they were practiced, by the cases handled at each level, and by the following descriptions:

LEVEL 1—Minimal Collaboration: Mental health and other healthcare providers work in separate facilities, have separate systems, and rarely communicate about cases.

LEVEL 2—Basic Collaboration at a Distance: Providers have separate systems at separate sites, but they engage in periodic communication about shared patients, mostly by telephone and through letters. Providers view each other as resources.

LEVEL 3—Basic Collaboration Onsite: Mental health and other healthcare professionals have separate systems, but they share facilities. Proximity supports occasional face-to-face meetings, and communication is improved and more regular.

LEVEL 4—Close Collaboration in a Partly Integrated System: Mental health and other healthcare providers share the same sites and have some systems in common, such as scheduling or charting. There are regular face-to-face interactions among primary care and behavioral health providers, coordinated treatment plans for difficult patients, and a basic understanding of each other's roles and cultures.

LEVEL 5—Close Collaboration in a Fully Integrated System: Mental health and other healthcare professionals share the same sites, vision, and systems. All providers are on the same team and have developed an in-depth understanding of each other's roles and areas of expertise.

This model does not suggest that all healthcare professionals need to engage in the higher levels of collaboration, but it outlines different types of collaborative effort to help providers and schools choose the level that best fits what they are trying to achieve (Doherty et al., 1996).

References

Biddle, B. J., & Berliner, D. C. (2002). Unequal School Funding in the United States. *Educational Leadership, 59*, 48–59.

Brock, S. E. (2015). Mental health matters. *Communiqué, 43*(7), 12–15.

Burns, B. J., Costello, E. J., Angold, A., Tweed, D., Stangl, D., Farmer, E. M., & Erkanli, A. (1995). Children's mental health service use across service sectors. *Health Affairs (Millwood), 14*(3), 147–159. https://doi.org/10.1377/hlthaff.14.3.147. PMID: 7498888.

Carr, E. G., Horner, R. H., Turnbull, A. P., Marquis, J. G., McLaughlin, D. M., McAtee, M. L., Smith, C. E., Ryan, K. A., Ruef, M. B., Doolabh, A., & Braddock, D. E. (1999). *Positive behavior support for people with developmental disabilities a research synthesis*. Distributed by ERIC Clearinghouse, https://eric.ed.gov/?id=ED439580

Centers for Disease Control and Prevention. (2018, September 14). *Health insurance portability and accounting act of 1996 (HIPAA)*. ttps://www.cdc.gov/phlp/publications/topic/hipaa.html

Clark, A. G., & Dockweiler, K. A. (2020). *Multi-tiered systems of support in elementary schools: The definitive guide to effective implementation and quality control*. Routledge Publishing.

Doggett, R. A., Bailey, J. D., & Johnson-Gros, K. N. (2008). Beyond crime and punishment: Reconceptualizing the school disciplinary ladder through a PBS model. *The Journal of Behavior Analysis of Offender and Victim Treatment and Prevention, 1*(3), 247–258. http://dx.doi.org/10.1037/h0100447

Doherty, W. J. (1995). The why's and levels of collaborative family health care. *Family Systems Medicine, 13*(3–4), 275–281. https://doi.org/10.1037/h0089174

Doherty, W. J., McDaniel, S. H., & Baird, M. A. (1996). Five levels of primary care/behavioral healthcare collaboration. *Behavioral Healthcare Tomorrow, 5*(5), 25–27.

Domitrovich, C. E., Bradshaw, C. P., Greenberg, M. T., Embry, D., Poduska, J. M., & Ialongo, N. S. (2010). Integrated models of school-based prevention: Logic and theory. *Psychology in the Schools, 47*(1), 71–88. https://doi.org/10.1002/pits.20452.

Eber, L., Malloy, Rose, J. M., & Flamini, A. (2014). School-based wraparound for adolescents. In H. Walker, & F. Gresham (Eds.), *Handbook of evidence-based practices for emotional and behavioral disorders* (pp. 378–393). Guilford Press.

Evans, S., T. Rybak, Strickland, H., & Owens, J. (2014). The Role of school mental health models in preventing and addressing children's emotional and behavioral problems. In H. Walker & F. Gresham (Eds.), *Handbook of evidence-based practices for emotional and behavioral disorders* (pp. 394–409). Guilford Press.

Gross, J., Mann, A., G., & Sulkowski, M. (2017). Helping homeless, foster care and juvenile justice students. *Communique, 45*(5), 1, 30–32.

Lewis, J. L., Sugai, G., & Colvin, G. (1998). Reducing problem behavior through a school-wide system of effective behavioral support: Investigation of a school-wide social skills training program and contextual interventions. *School Psychology Review, 27*(3), 446–459. https://doi.org/10.1080/02796015.1998.12085929

McDaniel, S. A. (2016). Why teamwork surpasses the individual approach. *Monitor,* 5.

Pollard, R. Q. Jr, Betts, W. R., Carroll, J. K., Waxmonsky, J. A., Barnett, S., DeGruy, F. V. 3rd, Pickler, L. L., & Kellar-Guenther, Y. (2014, May–June). Integrating primary care and behavioral health with four special populations: Children with special needs, people with serious mental illness, refugees, and deaf people. *American Psychologist, 69*(4), 377–387. https://doi.org/10.1037/a0036220.

Romano, J. L. (2015). *Prevention psychology: Enhancing personal and social well-being.* The American Psychological Association. www.apa.org/pubs/books/4317347?tab=1

Romano, J. L., & Hage, S. M. (2000). Prevention and counseling psychology: Revitalizing commitments for the 21st century. *The Counseling Psychologist, 28*(6), 733–763. https://doi.org/10.1177/0011000000286001

Sander, J. B. (2010). School psychology, juvenile justice, and the school to prison pipeline. *National Association of School Psychologists Communiqué,* 4–6.

Seeley, J., Severson, H., & Fixsen, A. (2014). Empirically based targeted prevention approaches for addressing externalizing and internalizing behavior disorders within school contexts. In H. Walker & F. Gresham (Eds.), *Handbook of evidence-based practices for emotional and behavioral disorders* (pp. 307–323). Guilford Press.

Strobach, K. V. (2018). Implementation of every student succeeds act: Update and next steps. *Communique', 46*(5), 9–11.

Sugai, G., & Horner, R. R. (2006). A promising approach for expanding and sustaining school-wide positive behavior support. *School Psychology Review, 35*(2), 245–259.

Weist, M., Stevens, R., Headley-Greenlaw, J., Miller, E., Fletcher, L., Collier, T., Arnau, P., Urbanski, J., Jenkins, J., & Diana, D. (2018). Expanded school mental health services: Development of the Southeastern School Behavioral Health Community. *Communique, 46*(8), 1, 18–20.

10

WHAT SHOULD SCHOOL-BASED MENTAL HEALTH PROFESSIONALS KNOW?

This chapter examines how Multi-tiered Systems of Support (MTSS), such as schoolwide positive behavior interventions and supports, can help schools develop partnerships between community-based providers, coordinate the mental health care for students who need it, and make sure that services are evidence-based and comprehensive. Teachers are at the front line of the MTSS process because they are typically the first school staff to interact with troubled students, to implement educational and/or behavioral interventions, and to seek the support of MTSS. To facilitate this process, the Every Student Succeeds Act (ESSA) has identified school counselors, psychologists, and social workers as the mental health providers in the school system. This chapter focuses on the unique contribution these school staff members can make to the MTSS process and, ultimately, children who are at risk of entering the school-to-prison pipeline.

Mental Health Providers in the School Setting

As is indicated in the previous chapter, ESSA has significantly reduced the authority of the Federal Secretary of Education, giving states and local jurisdictions substantial control over the implementation of academic standards, the design and enforcement of accountability systems, and the allocation of federal dollars. In addition, ESSA has defined who it considers to be the mental health providers in the public school setting, including state-licensed or state-certified school counselors, school psychologists, school social workers, or other state-licensed or certified mental health professionals qualified under state law to provide mental health services to children and adolescents. In part, ESSA has also described how mental health care should be delivered by recommending that these services be coordinated, comprehensive, and include community-school partnerships (NASP, 2021). As is indicated throughout this book, children with mental, emotional, and behavioral (MEB) health problems are scattered through multiple systems, including schools, foster homes, group homes, juvenile detention facilities, substance abuse agencies, and even prisons. To further compound this problem, many children with MEBs are never seen by the mental health system, which is a challenge for system-of-care models in offering a continuum of integrated mental health prevention services.

Balkanization of services and difficulties associated with pooling resources have in the past severely limited the implementation and coordination of systems of care for children in many communities (Hoagwood & Koretz, 1996), but an MTSS such as schoolwide positive behavior interventions and supports (SWPBIS) could mitigate these challenges. How to develop partnerships, coordinate mental health care for students, and make sure services are evidence-based and comprehensive will involve the efforts of teachers and other school staff members. However, ESSA's definition of mental health providers within the school system has solidified one of the critical roles of school counselors, school psychologists, and school social workers in ensuring that students with mental health needs receive this support.

SWPBIS, School Counselors, Psychologists, and Social Workers

School counselors, psychologists, and social workers are essential at Tier 3 of the SWPBIS for students with mental, emotional, and behavioral (MEB) health problems or disorders to ensure these students' parents or caretakers are aware of their child's mental health needs and the importance of interventions. As is indicated in Chapter 9, Tier 3 interventions provide highly individualized and specialized support systems for high-risk students, with the goal of reducing the severity and intensity of these problems. The SWPBIS model includes teams of professionals involved in the decision-making process that support and manage the provision of services within and outside the school system.

In many school systems, the school counselor is appointed by the school principal as chair or coordinator of SWPBIS teams and is the person teachers (and administrators) go to when they have concerns about a student's development or social, academic, mental, emotional, or behavioral health needs. Typically, school counselors are a permanent fixture of the school staff, which means they are on the school campus throughout the day and have access to administrators, teachers, parents, students, and student support members such as nurses, school psychologists, and social workers. Counselors also usually have access to confidential student records, including group testing data, school history, and the child's socioeconomic level and living situation. As coordinator, the school counselor may also schedule meetings to address a child's progress or lack thereof through the SWPBIS process with parents, teachers, school psychologists, and social workers.

Historically, school psychologists have been linked to special education, especially when a child is being considered for eligibility and support because of an emotional and behavioral disorder (EBD or ED). An EBD classification in educational settings allows schools to provide special education and related services to students who meet eligibility criteria. These criteria typically include the implementation of a variety of interventions over an extended period of time to which the student has not responded to adequately. Psychological screenings of the student's intelligence, academic skills, and mental, emotional, and behavioral development are frequently administered. A comprehensive psychological evaluation, along with an eligibility meeting, may follow, as well as special education support. Only about 1% of students with emotional and behavioral disorders are identified for special education services (U.S. Department of Education, 2007), but the prevalence literature finds that a minimum of 12% of students with MEB problems need services at any given time, and at least a third of all students will have experienced an MEB disorder at some point during their school years (Forness et al.,

2012). Since prevalence estimates indicate that most students with emotional and behavioral disorders do not qualify for special education services, their needs must be supported by the general education community within an MTSS.

When addressing children's mental health needs in the regular education environment, many teachers perceive themselves as not having sufficient expertise and training. In addition, teachers typically view school psychologists as having a primary role in most aspects of mental health service delivery in schools, including conducting screenings and behavioral assessments, monitoring student progress, and referring children to school-based or community services. This research also indicates that teachers cite insufficient coaching, unclear guidelines about the roles of different disciplines, and the absence of prevention efforts as barriers to the provision of adequate school-based mental health services (Reinke et al., 2011). Similarly, early childhood personnel report the need for increased training to better respond to the needs of young children in their classrooms and centers (Friedman-Krauss et al., 2014).

The introduction of pre-kindergarten (or Pre-K/PK), which is a classroom-based preschool program for children below the age of five, has given many children social, behavioral, and educational advantages in comparison to those children who have not received this support. Children entering pre-kindergarten have also increased the number of very young children entering school. As of 2016–2017, a total of 44 states, plus the District of Columbia, provide at least some state funding for Pre-K programs (Diffey et al., 2017), but this number is expected to increase under the current president's educational initiatives. Increasingly, younger children who display behavior patterns that stress the management skills of teachers and disrupt peer relations are also now entering school through the Pre-K programs (Seeley et al., 2014).

In an article about the development of the mental, emotional, and behavioral challenges of young children, Brauner and Stephens (2006) wrote that before there is thought and language, there is emotion, and it is this early effect within the context of the earliest relationships that forms the basis for all future development. The importance of emotional health in preparing young children to engage in cognitive tasks cannot be overstated because mature acts of deviance are now being committed by young children who are highly aggressive, oppositional, and very destructive in their social behavior toward others (Loeber et al., 2000). As is indicated in Chapter 4, comorbidity studies examining behavior problems have revealed that early aggressive behavior greatly increases the risk of conduct disorder, drug use, and other externalizing behaviors. When implemented in preschool, MTSS aids in the early identification of at-risk youth, minimizes inappropriate special education referrals, and remedies potential delays affecting school readiness and later learning or social-emotional outcomes (Greenwood et al., 2019).

As is indicated in Chapter 6, the biopsychosocial approach to behavioral healthcare involves the clinical application of both behavioral science and professional ethics to address behavioral health needs and promote biopsychosocial functioning. This approach recognizes the interactions between the biological, psychological, and sociocultural factors (Melchert, 2015), which makes the Comprehensive Behavioral Healthcare Assessment for Children and Adolescents (introduced in Chapter 7) a very useful tool in understanding these dynamics and developing behavioral support plans that address risks, protective factors, and needs. The support of school social workers is essential in the use of this questionnaire during Tier 3 of SWPBIS, especially for minoritized youth and those children who are at risk for the school-to-prison pipeline. School social workers are also vital when it comes to communicating with a child's parents or caretakers. As is indicated in the previous chapter, the public school system has historically been identified for its role in educating students, but it has also become the front line of prevention for children with MEB health problems or disorders. As is indicated in Chapter 7, parents and caretakers may not understand the importance of the MTSS as a prevention tool in the school system, which the social worker can clarify. Like school psychologists, there are typically social workers in the school system and also within the community. If the student is in foster care or involved with a community-based program, having similarly trained staff members in both settings can be advantageous. These individuals typically have a common language, ethical guidelines, training, and experience, which can eliminate barriers to communicating and accessing resources.

With the growing interest in schoolwide organizational models like SWPBIS, there is an opportunity for integrating a continuum of increasingly intensive prevention programs and services for students. The components of comprehensive prevention and early intervention services may vary based on the needs of the population of students served, but the success of these services relies on educators, school-employed mental health professionals, other specialized instructional support personnel, and community health and mental health providers working seamlessly across an MTSS. This seamless coordination of services does not jeopardize the safety of students, teachers, or schools, which is another advantage.

Effective School–Community Partnership to Support School Mental Health

On June 17, 2021, the National Association of School Psychologists (NASP) and National Center for School Mental Health (NCSMH) wrote that successful and sustainable school mental health systems integrate partners seamlessly so the full spectrum of mental health supports and services are tightly coordinated to meet student needs. Effective collaboration between school staff and community mental health partners broadens the availability of supports and enhances access to mental health care. However, as is indicated in the previous chapter, the roles and responsibilities of school and community partners will differ based on the unique resources and needs of school districts and the local community.

According to NASP and NCSMH (2021), the allocation of roles and responsibilities for school- and community-employed personnel across an MTSS at Tier 3 will be implemented primarily by community professionals with support from school-employed mental health professionals and other relevant specialized instructional support personnel. The following are the key elements identified by NASP and NCSMH of school–community partnerships and specific action steps for states, districts, and communities to foster effective collaboration between the schools, community, and behavioral health partners.

Element I: Appropriate Staffing of School and Community Mental Health Professionals

Most professional associations have recommended staffing ratios to deliver comprehensive wellness promotion, prevention, early identification, and intervention services at the student, classroom, and school-wide levels. The nationally recommended ratios of school-employed mental health professionals for school counselors are 1:250, school psychologists 1:500, and school social workers 1:250. In a recent article in *Education Week* (Riser-Kositsky, 2022), however, it was reported that more than 5.4 million public school students (12%) attend districts with no psychologists, and almost half a million students (1%) attend districts with no school counselors.

Element II: Clear Roles and Responsibilities

Partnerships between school and community mental health providers are facilitated by a clear delineation of roles and responsibilities. The use of a memorandum of understanding or other agreements to detail the terms of the partnership, a shared language and accountability system that is grounded in a mutual set of goals, and a communication plan between school- and community-employed staff, families, and other relevant stakeholders is an essential step.

Element III: Funding to Support School-Community Mental Health Partnerships

Successful school-community mental health partnerships are funded by an array of sources, including legislative authorizations and federal block grants (e.g., the Healthy Schools, Healthy Communities Program; Project AWARE; state education agency grants; Promoting Student Resilience Program; and Title XX Social Services Block Grant), state or county funding (e.g., budget line items, local taxes, and funding to implement special programs), fee-for-service revenue from third-party payers (e.g., State Children's Health Insurance Programs, Medicaid), and private individual donors and foundations (e.g., Annie E. Casey Foundation and Robert Wood Johnson Foundation).

As is indicated earlier, successful and sustainable school mental health systems leverage and integrate the strengths and resources of school-employed and community mental health partners. Partners are chosen based on their ability to meet the needs of troubled children, and these partnerships should be routinely evaluated for their effectiveness and contribution to the overall improvement of agreed upon shared goals (NASP & NCSMH, 2021).

Equity-focused SWPBIS Reduces Racial Inequalities in School Discipline

As is indicated in Chapter 1, African American children frequently receive harsher discipline for the same behaviors that White children display in the school system. But is there evidence that SWPBIS can reduce racial inequalities in school discipline? This question was researched in a scientific study conducted by McIntosh et al. in 2021. During this study, the effects of a whole-school equity intervention were implemented, using a SWPBIS framework in eight elementary schools with inequitable referrals of African American students. The intervention involved assessing patterns of racial disparities in school discipline decisions and providing professional development on adapting school-wide behavior systems to improve cultural responsiveness. Results indicated that schools receiving the intervention significantly decreased racial disparities in school discipline and rates of office discipline referrals for African American students.

ESSA, SWPBIS, NASP Practice Model, and the School-to-Prison Pipeline

The importance of addressing all of the steps identified in this and the previous chapter to ensure that all troubled children receive the mental help support they need cannot be overstated, especially for those children who are at risk for entering the school-to-prison pipeline (STPP). As is indicated in Chapter 1, the rate of incarceration of African American youth in the United States is not a new or equal opportunity problem. It dates back to chattel slavery (when it was legal to enslave and own human beings as property), lynch laws, and convict lease and peonage systems. These diabolical methods of detaining and subjugating African Americans have made the STPP one of the longest and most heinous moral and ethical social justice challenges this country has faced.

The STPP is a complex biopsychosocial problem that is impacted by institutions (e.g., courts, schools), social conditions (e.g., poverty, access to mental health care), and biological and psychological factors (e.g., one's developmental status, mental health, and the social construct we call race). Because the STPP is inextricably linked to schools, school staff are a key component to its demise. To accomplish this, school staff should be committed to supporting ongoing dialogue and self-reflection about antiracism, equity, diversity, inclusion, and social justice, especially in schools where a disproportionate number of African American students are disciplined. A common comment among White and even African American educators is that they are not racist. But this idea has been challenged by Kendi (2019), author of the book *How to Be an Antiracist*. For Kendi, "racist" is not a descriptive but a pejorative word expressing a negative or disrespectful connotation, a low opinion, or a lack of respect toward someone or something. The opposite of racist is not "not racist" but "antiracist." For example, a person with a racist perspective believes that problems such as the STPP are rooted in groups of people, thus allowing racial inequalities like this pipeline to persist. An antiracist, however, confronts this racial inequality and seeks to prevent it.

For school psychologists, the NASP Model for Comprehensive and Integrated School Psychological Services (also known as the NASP Practice Model) represents the National Association of School Psychologist's (NASP) official policy regarding the delivery of school psychological services. The NASP Practice Model went into effect July 1, 2020, and is one of four major parts of NASP's 2020 Professional Standards. The other three national standards include Principles for Professional Ethics, Standards for Graduate Preparation of School Psychologists, and Standards for the Credentialing of School Psychologists. This model clearly indicates that school psychologists have an ethical and professional responsibility to attend to issues of equity, diversity, and inclusion in their professional practice, as well as advocate to eliminate systemic racism, inequality, and other discriminatory factors in schools that can harm or marginalize students (NASP, 2021; National Association of School Psychologists, 2021). Along with personal efforts in confronting one's own explicit and implicit biases toward African Americans and other people of color, these are "antiracist" prevention strategies.

References

Brauner, C. B., & Stephens, C. B. (2006, May–June). Estimating the prevalence of early childhood serious emotional/behavioral disorders: Challenges and recommendations. *Public Health Reports, 121*(3), 303–310. https://doi.org/10.1177/003335490612100314. PMID: 16640155; PMCID: PMC1525276.

Diffey, L., Parker, E., & Atchison, B. (2017). *State pre-K funding 2016–17 fiscal year: Trends and opportunities. education commission of the states.* www.ecs.org/wp-content/uploads/State-Pre-K-Funding-2016-17-Fiscal-Year-Trends-and-opportunities-1.pdf

Forness, S. R., Freeman, S. F., Paparella, T., Kauffman, J. M., & Walker, H. M. (2012). Special education implications of point and cumulative prevalence for children with emotional or behavioral disorders. *Journal of Emotional and Behavioral Disorders, 20*, 4–18.

Friedman-Krauss, A. H., Raver, C. C., Neuspiel, J. M., & Kinsel, J. (2014). Child behavior problems, teacher executive functions, and teacher stress in head start classrooms. *Early Education and Development, 25*(5), 681–702. https://doi.org/10.1080/10409289.2013.825190

Greenwood, C. R., Carta, J. J., Schnitz, A. G., Irvin, D. W., Jia, F., & Atwater, J. (2019). Filling an information gap in preschool MTSS and RTI decision making. *Exceptional Children, 85*(3), 271–290. https://doi.org/10.1177/0014402918812473

Griffiths, C. M., & Sullivan, N. (2022, August 19). In schools, honest talk about racism can reduce discrimination. *Scientific American.* www.scientificamerican.com/article/in-schools-honest-talk-about-racism-can-reduce-discrimination/

Hoagwood, K., & Koretz, D. (1996). Embedding prevention services within systems of care: Strengthening the nexus for children. *Applied and Preventive Psychology, 5*(4), 225–234. https://doi.org/10.1016/S0962-1849(96)80014-X. ISSN: 0962-1849

Kendi, I. X. (2019). *How to be an antiracist.* One World.

Loeber, R., Farrington, D. P., & Mcglynn, M. M. (2000). Serious and violent juvenile offenders: Risk factors and successful interventions. *Behavioral Disorders, 25*(4), 374–375. https://doi.org/10.1177/019874290002500406

McIntosh, K. T., Girvan, E. J., Fairbanks Falcon, S., McDaniel, S. C., Smolkowski, K., Bastable, E., Santiago-Rosario, M. R., Izzard, S., Austin, S. C., Nese, R. N. T., & Baldy, T. S. (2021). Equity-focused PBIS approach reduces racial inequities in school discipline: A randomized controlled trial. *School Psychology, 36*(6), 433–444. https://doi.org/10.1037/spq0000466. PMID: 34766811.

Melchert, T. P. (2015). *Biopsychosocial practice: A science-based framework for behavioral healthcare.* The American Psychological Association. www.apa.org/pubs/books/4317346.html

NASP. (2021, November 18). *Every student succeeds act: Details of the new law.* www.nasponline.org/research-and-policy/policy-priorities/relevant-law/the-every-student-succeeds-act/details-of-essa

NASP & NCSMH. (2021, June 17). *Effective school-community partnerships to support school mental health.* www.schoolmentalhealth.org/media/SOM/Microsites/NCSMH/Documents/Resources/Effective-School-Comm-Partnerships-to-support-SMH-Final.pdf

National Association of School Psychologists. (2021, November). *The importance of addressing equity, diversity, and inclusion in schools: Dispelling myths about critical race theory [handout].* https://www.nasponline.org/resources-and-publications/resources-and-podcasts/diversity-and-social-justice/social-justice/the-importance-of-addressing-equity-diversity-and-inclusion-in-schools-dispelling-myths-about-critical-race-theory

Reinke, W. M., Stormont, M., Herman, K. C., Puri, R., & Goel, N. (2011). Supporting children's mental health in schools: Teacher perceptions of needs, roles, and barriers. *School Psychology Quarterly, 26*(1), 1–13. https://doi.org/10.1037/a0022714

Riser-Kositsky, M. (2022, March 28). Data: Does your state have enough school psychologists and counselors? *Education Week.* www.edweek.org/leadership/data-does-your-state-have-enough-school-psychologists-and-counselors/2022/03

Seeley, J., Severson, H., & Fixsen, A. (2014). Empirically based targeted prevention approaches for addressing externalizing and internalizing behavior disorders within school contexts. In H. Walker & F. Gresham (Eds.), *Handbook of evidence-based practices for emotional and behavioral disorders* (pp. 307–323). Guilford Press.

U.S. Department of Education. (2007). *Twenty-seventh annual report to Congress on implementation of the Individuals with Disabilities Education Act.* U. S. Department of Education

SECTION V

MAPPING AN AGENDA FOR THE FUTURE OF ALL YOUTH

11

MAPPING AN AGENDA FOR THE FUTURE OF ALL YOUTH BY APPLYING PSYCHOLOGY TO FUNDAMENTAL PROBLEMS

This chapter provides a brief summary of this book's contents by examining how prevention science can play a pivotal role in preventing the school-to-prison pipeline (STPP). It does this by reviewing the history of the STPP and this history's continued impact on the lives of vulnerable African American children. Included in this review is a list of some of the tools needed to intervene. These tools include changes in the dysfunctional narrative regarding children with mental, emotional, and behavioral health problems; attention to and elimination of explicit and implicit biases in observers; and the utilization of a public health approach in the school system that focuses on early detection and mental health promotion and prevention.

It may seem untimely and ill-considered to publish a book about the school-to-prison pipeline (STPP) when so many public schools are just reopening because of the COVID-19 pandemic. But as Americans witnessed and responded to COVID-19 protocols and read or listened to news updates about this pandemic's local, state, national, and international impact, they also watched the murder of George Floyd, Breonna Taylor, and others by police, and violent hate crimes such as the brutal slaying of Ahmaud Arbery by three racist White men as he jogged through a neighborhood. These bitter revelations about racism in the United States during a time when everyone should have been working together to battle a virus that could destroy the human race have sparked questions about how far this country has come in its treatment of African Americans and other people of color. Some sentiments of those revelations were captured recently in *The School Psychologist ("The dual pandemics of COVID-19 and systemic racism: Navigating our path forward")* by Jones (2021) when she wrote that this pandemic has shined a magnifying glass on racially based structural inequalities in a manner that was impossible to look away from. This pandemic has also revealed the ways in which political and economic forces have a direct impact on the lives and health of every human, with the ultimate consequence of deep-seated social, economic, and educational inequalities. These deep-seated social, economic, and educational inequalities directly affected the distribution of healthcare risks and resources and revealed the disproportionate impact these inequalities can have on racially diverse communities (Gravlee, 2020).

The social, economic, and educational inequalities have, however, spawned national and international movements for social justice, such as "Black Lives Matter," and painful but honest discussions about how to heal a nation from centuries of greed, corroded social, spiritual, and moral values, racial terrorism, violence, murder with impunity, and inconceivable human oppression against African Americans and other people of color. These discussions have also created opportunities for all Americans to consciously reflect on the ideals of this country and how these ideals can be realized and implemented. As is indicated in *The Sum of Us: What Racism Costs Everyone and How We Can Prosper Together* (McGhee, 2021), these discussions and movements are not (as some may believe) only beneficial to African Americans. Instead, they are essential for all Americans, especially its children who have not even been born.

The American Psychological Association, which has for 130 years embraced racist views (as cited in Haggert, 2022), is currently embroiled in these conscious reflections as well. For instance, the American Psychological Association (APA) recently apologized to communities of color for its role in promoting, perpetuating, and failing to challenge racism. The APA has also acknowledged the role racism plays in all aspects of society and resolved to combat racism and work toward its elimination (Worrell, 2022). In addition, APA's CEO, Arthur C. Evans Jr., joined

American Psychiatric Association CEO, Saul Levin, and National Association of Social Workers CEO, Angelo McClain, in expressing concern regarding COVID-19's disproportionate and devastating impact on African Americans, as well as systemic racism. "As mental-health professionals," they said, "we've seen firsthand how devastating systemic racism can be on the mental health of people of color." African Americans are more likely to experience stress, anxiety, and depression than Whites, yet they're much less likely to have access to adequate mental health care. These three organizations committed to taking steps to ending systemic racism, which they indicated must be a public health priority requiring immediate action (American Psychological Association, 2020).

As is indicated in Chapter 1, racial disparities in the application of school discipline in public schools have been documented for many years, and these disparities most frequently result in juvenile court referrals of African American youth (Wald & Kurlaender, 2003). The rate of incarceration of African American youth in the United States dates back to chattel slavery, the lynch laws, and convict lease and peonage systems. These diabolical methods of detaining and subjugating African Americans make the school-to-prison pipeline (STPP) one of the longest and most heinous moral and ethical social justice challenges this country faces. Systemic racism, in its various forms, is one reason why the STPP has continued to exist and why it has remained such an intractable yet preventable problem. Therefore, it is encouraging that the American Psychological, American Psychiatric Association, and National Association of Social Workers have taken steps to end systemic racism.

This book, however, describes the STPP as a complex biopsychosocial problem, which is influenced by biological, psychological, and social factors (e.g., systemic racism). It also provides some of the tools needed to intervene in this diabolical problem. These tools include such things as changes in the current dysfunctional narrative about children with mental, emotional, and behavioral health problems (including post-traumatic stress disorder), confronting and addressing explicit and implicit biases (which the best educated and ethical mental health provider is not immune to), and utilizing the public health approach for children who are at risk for entering the STPP, which focuses on early detection and mental health promotion and prevention.

There are certainly structural and individual challenges in some public-school systems, such as systemic racism, but this system is considered the front line of prevention for children with mental, emotional, and behavioral health problems. The Every Student Succeeds Act has given schools and mental health providers, such as school psychologists, counselors, and social workers, an unprecedented opportunity to ensure that children have access to mental health support, which is especially important with the added stressors at home, school, and within the community due to COVID-19. This can partially be accomplished using problem-solving teams or Multi-tiered Systems of Support (MTSS), such as schoolwide positive behavior intervention and supports (SWPBIS), and these supports can be embedded seamlessly into public schools without jeopardizing safety.

Embedding MTSS, such as SWPBIS, into the public school system brings mental health practitioners and the schools one step closer to realizing Romano and Hage's expanded five-part definition of prevention. This definition includes stopping a problem from ever occurring, delaying the onset of an age-related problem, intervening with those at risk for a problem, reducing the impact of an existing problem, strengthening knowledge, attitudes, behaviors, and skills of individuals or groups to enhance protections against problems and disorders, and supporting and advocating for institutional, community, and government policies that promote physical and emotional health and well-being (2000). Ultimately, however, preventing the STPP can only be accomplished by everyday people at the local level, working together with and for their communities.

References

American Psychological Association. (2020, August 24). *APA calls for comprehensive policy changes to end the US racism pandemic*. www.apaservices.org/advocacy/news/end-racism-pandemic

Gravlee, C. C. (2020). Systemic racism, chronic health inequities, and COVID-19: A syndemic in the making? *American Journal of Human Biology: The Official Journal of the Human Biology Council, 32*(5), e23482. https://doi.org/10.1002/ajhb.23482

Haggert, M. (2022, March). 4 questions for Linda James Myers. *Monitor on Psychology*, by Maryann Haggert, vol. 53, no. 2. https://www.apa.org/monitor/2022/03/conversation-myers

Jones, J. M. (2021). The dual pandemics of COVID-19 and systemic racism: Navigating our path forward. *The School Psychologist, 36*(5), 427–431. https://doi.org/10.1037/spq0000472

McGhee, H. (2021). *The sum of us: What racism costs everyone and how we can prosper together*. One World.

Romano, J. L., & Hage, S. M. (2000). Prevention and counseling psychology: Revitalizing commitments for the 21st century. *The Counseling Psychologist, 28*(6), 733–763. https://doi.org/10.1177/0011000000286001

Wald, J., & Kurlaender, M. (2003). Connected in Seattle? An exploratory study of student perceptions of discipline and attachments to teachers. In J. Wald & D. Losen (Eds.), *New directions for youth development* (pp. 35–54). Jossey-Bass. https://doi.org/10.1002/yd.53. PMID: 14635433.

Worrell, F. C. (2022, January/February). *Monitor on Psychology*, vol. 53, no. 1. https://www.apa.org/monitor/2022/01/pc

INDEX

For Product Safety Concerns and Information please contact our EU
representative GPSR@taylorandfrancis.com
Taylor & Francis Verlag GmbH, Kaufingerstraße 24, 80331 München, Germany